EXPLORING GOD'S WORD

BIBLE GUIDE TO
EPHESIANS, PHILIPPIANS AND
COLOSSIANS

EXPLORING GOD'S WORD

BIBLE GUIDE TO EPHESIANS, PHILIPPIANS AND COLOSSIANS

Donald Guthrie

HODDER AND STOUGHTON
LONDON   SYDNEY   AUCKLAND   TORONTO

British Library Cataloguing in Publication Data

Guthrie, Donald
 Exploring god's word
 Bible guide to Ephesians, Philippians,
 Colossians. – (Hodder Christian paperback)
 1. Bible. N. T. Ephesians – Commentaries
 2. Bible. N. T. Philippians – Commentaries
 3. Bible. N. T. Colossians – Commentaries
 I. Title
 227'.506   BS2695.3

ISBN 0 340 34498 9

Contents

Chapter 2

Chapter 3

Chapter 4

Chapter 5

Chapter 6

PHILIPPIANS

Introduction

Chapter 1

Chapter 2

Chapter 3

Chapter 4

COLOSSIANS

Chapter 1

Chapter 2

Preface

The reader might be interested to know what prompted the writing of this series of Bible Guides. It arose from a desire to promote more expositional study of the biblical text.

I had frequently had recourse to the Pulpit Commentary for suggestions for homiletical structures, but recognised the need for something more concise and relevant. The present series presents a collection of outlines on which it is hoped that the reader will be able to build. Only those outlines which arise naturally out of the text itself have been included.

I am grateful to the publishers who at every stage have encouraged me in the conception and working out of the project.

General Introduction •

The purpose of these guides is to provide a tool for the expositional study of the biblical text. There are many different approaches to the study of Scripture, but our aim will be to begin with the scriptural text with the purpose of discovering what contribution it can make to the life of the Christian.

Each guide consists of a number of outlines which are designed to assist the Bible student to gain an orderly understanding of the content and meaning of the text. It is hoped that this will provide an exciting field of study. Although the aim is exegetical, that is, to discover what the text actually says, the need to see how the text can be personally applied to daily life has been a major factor in the production of the outlines. In personal study, in group study and for homiletical purposes there is no substitute for the orderly presentation of the Scriptures.

Each biblical book is split into sections. For each selection of verses, different outlines are provided, one or two for the whole section and others for smaller parts. These are arranged in order according to the starting verse of each section. A glance at the table of contents will clearly demonstrate this arrangement.

Some overlapping within the outlines is unavoidable, but the various combinations illustrate the different approaches that can be made to the text.

It is hoped that the outlines provided will serve as a catalyst for the development of other outlines.

EPHESIANS
Introduction

About Ephesus
This was the capital of the Roman province of Asia. It had, however, seen more flourishing days, but was now on the decline. It was nevertheless still an influential centre, especially for a wide variety of religious ideas. The most dominant of these was the cult of Aphrodite, which was attended by immoral practices.

About the church
We know from the book of Acts that Paul spent three years at Ephesus, during which time a strong Christian witness was established in this strategic city. We would expect as a result that Paul would have reflected more intimate knowledge of his readers than is seen in this epistle, and this has led to the theory that the epistle was sent to several churches as a kind of circular. If this is correct, Ephesus was the church that preserved the letter. Some texts do not refer to Ephesus in 1:1 and this evidence would support the circular theory.

About the purpose of the letter
There is no direct indication of purpose in the letter itself. In view of the close parallels with Colossians it is most likely that Ephesians is intended as a general antidote for the kind of tendency which is specifically combatted in Colossians. The main aim is both doctrinal and moral, the first part setting out the doctrine of Christ and the church, and the second containing advice on the Christian life.

About the writer

This is a letter from prison. In it Paul brings out some profound Christian truths. Some regard it as one of Paul's most doctrinal letters. Although he does not reveal so much about himself in this letter as in some others (e.g. 2 Corinthians and Philippians), there are plenty of personal insights. Some scholars have maintained that Paul was not the author of this epistle, but the grounds for disputing his authorship are not as strong as those which affirm it. The early Christian testimony strongly supports it.

About the date

If Ephesians was written about the same time as Colossians, it is most probable that a date towards the end of Paul's Roman imprisonment should be adopted, perhaps A.D. 60. The alternative suggestion that Colossians was written during an Ephesian imprisonment would also support an early date for Ephesians.

EPHESIANS 1:1, 2
Christian greetings

The way Paul begins his letters is always
instructive.
It tells us something about both writer and readers.

The Author

Paul does not need to identify himself further, for all would
know the name of the great missionary to the Gentiles. But
he does describe his function.

  (a) *An apostle*. In this he compares with those appointed
      by Jesus.
  (b) *Of Jesus Christ*. Paul's whole life was devoted to
      serving Christ. He was an apostle sent by Jesus
      Christ.
  (c) *By the will of God*. Paul was deeply conscious that
      God had overruled his life, from his conversion, and
      throughout his missionary call.

The Readers

Some texts include the words 'in Ephesus'. Some omit
them. If the readers were not in Ephesus they must have
been in the same general area.

  (a) They are called *saints*. This means 'holy ones' and is
      used by Paul of all believers. It speaks of the target
      rather than the achievement.
  (b) They are also described as '*faithful in Christ Jesus*'.
      The faithful are here those who have exercised faith,
      i.e. believers. Their being 'in Christ' points to the
      source of their spiritual life.

The Greeting

Grace has a special significance for Christians. It speaks of God's free provision for man's needs.

Peace points to the result of God's gracious action. Man may have peace with God.

Both grace and peace are said to be from God. He is described as a God of grace (1 Pet. 5:10) and a God of peace (Heb. 13:20).

Both are also said to be from Christ. Grace comes from Christ (John 1:17) and he is our peace (Eph. 2:14).

Is this the kind of blessing we would wish for others?
Do they see in us evidence of grace and peace?

EPHESIANS 1:1, 2
The highest things in the world

The greatest things are spiritual, not temporal.

The highest office in the world
  (a) The apostle was a messenger of the greatest person.
  (b) He was the bearer of the greatest message.
  (c) He was called to the greatest calling – the will of God.

The highest characters in the world
  (a) *The holy ones.* These are people destined for the greatest moral excellence.
  (b) *Faithful.* This indicates dependence on God.

The highest blessing in the world
Christian grace and peace are not natural possessions. They are provisions of the Christian gospel.

These things are open to all Christians.
They should challenge us to possess them.

EPHESIANS 1:3–10
The church

*Although there is no specific reference to the
church, the use of 'we' and 'us' indicates the people
of God. Moreover, the church is mentioned
several times elsewhere in the epistle.*

The church originates in God's love

It is not the result of human organisation. Man was not
consulted about its development. It all began with God.
Since God is love his purposes express his love (verse 5).

Paul sees the church as chosen:

(a) Chosen *for God*. Choice is influenced generally by
desire.

(b) Chosen *in Christ*. Christ is God's chosen servant
(Isa. 42:1), and we are chosen by the same God.

(c) Chosen *eternally*. Chosen by God before we could
choose for ourselves.

(d) Chosen *to be holy*. God desired that his people
should be as holy as he is.

The church consists of adopted sons

'To be his sons' goes beyond creation. In one sense all are
children of God through creation. But this is sonship of a
different kind.

(a) Adoption is *predetermined*. All along God had planned a community of sons.

(b) The *means* was also predetermined. It was through
Christ. God planned this before man revolted
against him.

(c) The *aim* was also predetermined. It was not only
through Christ, but for him.

(d) Adoption was governed by *what pleased God*. We
are assured that our new status is according to God's
good pleasure. What pleases him must surely please
us.

(e) Adoption *magnifies God's grace*. There is no honouring of the sons – only of the one who makes
sonship possible.

The church is a redeemed community

Closely allied to the theme of adoption is the theme of redemption. The root idea is deliverance from a state of bondage.

(a) We are *redeemed in him*. There is no other name by which it can be achieved.

(b) We are redeemed *at great cost*. The blood of Christ points to his sacrificial death. Redemption always involves cost.

(c) Because we are redeemed we are *forgiven*. This takes sin seriously. Trespasses are side-steps and forgiveness sets our feet on the right road again.

(d) The redeemed owe everything to *divine grace*. God's grace is given unstintingly.

(e) Grace leads to *wisdom and insight*. God does not leave us in the dark.

(f) The completion of God's purposes in redemption is *certain but still future*.

Here is a high view of God's community.
It is seen as the aim of God's carefully designed plan.
How highly do we value it?

EPHESIANS 1:3–6
The blessings of the gospel

Paul begins this letter with some profound
statements about the gospel.

The source of the blessings

The whole process begins with a heavenly father. His fatherliness is first seen in relation to Jesus Christ.

He acts in the same way towards us, by bestowing blessings on us. But why in heavenly places? This is to distinguish the blessings from earthly benefits.

The motive behind the blessings

Paul is sure that everything proceeds from love. He stresses this again in 2:4. The love motive is central in Paul's thought of God. Cf. Rom. 5:8 – which speaks of God's love overcoming man's enmity.

The planning of the blessings

Paul does not hesitate to speak of God choosing and planning. Predestination for him is no more than carrying out his designs.

'Before the foundation of the world' points to the perfect and therefore unchangeable character of God's will.

The choice of the recipients

The statement 'he chose me' is meant to be reassuring, not off-putting. Why get bogged down with free will when the intention is to point out that believers are the special objects of God's care?

The purpose, however, is demanding – nothing less than to make us holy and blameless.

The new status of the recipients

Believers are sons through Jesus Christ. This is in total contrast with man's natural environment. But this exalted status is the purpose of God – what he wills for us.

All this leads Paul to praise God for his grace. It also leads him to refer to Christ as the 'Beloved'. All Christians may and should praise God in a similar way.

EPHESIANS 1:3
Thanking God for his blessings

It is Paul's usual procedure to begin with praise to God.

Christians enjoy many blessings

Every Christian is in a favoured position. God delights to bless us. Note that here Paul uses the past tense to express a present reality.

Their blessings are spiritual

This marks them out from material blessings. Prosperity in this life is not the target for the Christian, although there is nothing against it.

What Paul is thinking of is possessions like peace, joy, love and gentleness.

The blessings are also heavenly

They are normal for the kingdom of heaven. They flourish among members of this kingdom. To be in such company is itself a rich blessing.

These blessings should lead to praise

'Praise be to God' should be the Christian's constant song.

Paul had no difficulty in finding subjects for praising God. To reflect on what God has done for us will lead to adoration.

EPHESIANS 1:4–6
God's plan for man

Paul helps us to look at man as God looks at him and intends him to be. It is difficult for most of us to look at things from God's point of view. It will not surprise us that Paul introduces here some profound thoughts.

God's plan was conceived before creation

To understand that plan we must reflect on the nature of God.

(a) Because he is *infinite*, his plan must include details.
(b) Because he is *eternal*, his plan can and does involve all future issues.

With such a plan there is no room for fluctuations. No event can take him by surprise.

God's plan was centred on man's holiness

This is not surprising. A holy God must desire a holy people.

The process of salvation involves transformation, i.e. sanctification. Paul refers to the new character before introducing the new status, i.e. becoming sons through Jesus Christ.

God's plan proceeds from his sovereignty and his love

Paul links together what are often separated with confusing results.

Love is the spring of God's election. God cannot act in an ungracious way.

God's *will* is always good. What he wills he performs.

This is most encouraging, to be sharply distinguished from fatalism.

When love is seen as sovereign love, and sovereignty is seen as loving power, each is better understood.

God's plan is a provision of his grace

Grace is undeserved favour. The plan of salvation is independent of man's achievements. Paul allows no place for merit.

> *It is important to recognise that God has a plan.*
> *His purposes are not always easy to understand,*
> *but the Christian must rest in the nature of his love.*

EPHESIANS 1:4
Election

> *This subject is usually considered difficult because*
> *God's choice seems to rule out human choice. Yet*
> *Paul does not hesitate to say that God chooses.*

Election centres in Christ

Everything revolves around Christ. The chosen are 'in Christ'.

Election is an expression of God's will
Paul speaks of the good pleasure of God. His will is never arbitrary or tyrannical.

Election took place in eternity
It happened before creation. It was ever present in the mind of God.

Election has the highest aim
Believers are chosen to be holy and blameless. There is no compromise here. The target is nothing short of perfection.

> *Election is intended to be both encouraging and challenging. Once recognised in this way, it sets before us the noblest aim.*

EPHESIANS 1:7–14
Redemption

> *This is one of Paul's most significant themes. It draws attention to Christ's mission as a rescue operation.*

Redemption brings many benefits
  (a) *Deliverance*. This is the root meaning of redemption. It implies a change of status from bondage to freedom.
  (b) *Forgiveness*. This means the removal of guilt. It is closely linked with, though separated from deliverance.
  (c) *Knowledge*. Man is no longer kept in the dark. He has been told the mystery of God's wonderful plan for him.
  (d) *Unity*. In no other way can everyone and everything be brought together. The unifying factor is Christ the head.
  (e) *Inheritance*. Paul frequently mentions this in his

letters. As with all Christian benefits, this centres in Christ. As a guarantee we are sealed with the Spirit.

Redemption has many facets

(a) *It is an act of grace.* Paul writes of the riches of God's grace (cf. 2:7). He knows that salvation is all of grace (2:8). This removes all cause for human pride.

(b) *It is an act of God's perfect will.* Paul acknowledges that this is a mystery. Even with revelation the knowledge of God's working must in some aspects remain a mystery. Nevertheless Paul is convinced that God is working to a plan.

(c) *It is an act which cost much.* It was 'through his blood', which means as a result of the death of Christ. Paul never ceases to wonder at the cost of our salvation. The cost idea is here incorporated in the idea of ransom.

(d) *It is an act which redounds to God's glory.* Note the repetition of the words 'to the praise of his glory'. With such great achievements who would be silent?

Since the redemption theme is so important it is appropriate that the redeemed should tell others about it.

EPHESIANS 1:7
A concise statement about redemption

Paul is a master of concise statements with profound meanings. This verse has a penetrating content.

The meaning of redemption

Redemption from the bondage of sin is in mind. It means release from the power as well as the penalty of sin.

The cost of redemption

The reference to the blood focusses attention on the sacrifice of Christ's life for our sake.

The motive of redemption

It all proceeds from the riches of grace. Grace points to divine initiative, not to man's designs.

There is no doubt that such redemption is worth having. The alternative is continued bondage.

EPHESIANS 1:7
Forgiveness

Forgiveness is a vital matter wherever people are convicted of sin. To those under the burden of guilt it is the sweetest sound.

The connection between forgiveness and Christ's blood

The close link comes out in Matt. 26:28. The death of Christ is the foundation of the offer of forgiveness. Compare Heb. 9:22 – 'without the shedding of blood there is no forgiveness of sins'.

The connection between forgiveness and atonement

Although closely linked these concepts are nevertheless separate. Atonement is one act, forgiveness is continuous. Forgiveness is the experiencing of God's saving work.

The connection between grace and forgiveness

Forgiveness is according to the riches of God's grace. It is important to be reminded that forgiveness is undeserved. There is no way that a person can earn it. It is God's free gift.

Paul talks about what we have if we are in Christ Jesus. Forgiveness is open to all who have faith. If

*we have not experienced it but desire it, we may
know that God desires to give it.*

EPHESIANS 1:9
A mystery unveiled

*Paul was fond of writing about the mystery of the
gospel. The solving of any mystery provides
endless fascination, none more so than the mystery
of God's dealing with mankind.*

There was a time when the mystery was veiled
Throughout the Old Testament age we find partial revelation.

So much pointed to Christ, but only after his incarnation
could the nature of the mystery be understood.

The unveiling of the mystery required wisdom
The whole plan of salvation is evidence of God's wisdom.

Paul expounds the wisdom theme in 1 Corinthians 1 and
2, where he contrasts God's wisdom with man's wisdom.

The mystery appears to many to be foolish. God supplies
spiritual wisdom and insight to enable us to grasp his
methods.

The mystery is an expression of God's will
So many fail to appreciate God's purpose. They think they
have understood because they fail to recognise it as a
mystery.

God's purpose in Christ needs more than human wisdom
to grasp it.

*Think what resources of understanding are
available to the Christian. How foolish it would be
not to make the most of them.*

EPHESIANS 1:10
Uniting everything in Christ

Paul sets his sights on the widest application of God's work in Christ. He sees a world at variance with itself. The most powerful influences today are still divisive. Paul's words here have relevance to our present situation.

Disunity rules apart from God's plan

It is a basic assumption that unity is desirable. Biblical revelation shows sin as a great divider. It is the great destroyer of unity. But it is God's intention to rectify the divisions.

What needs to be united

We may note the various spheres in which unity is needed.

(a) The uniting of *sinful people to God*. The major chasm is caused by sin which alienates people from God. The act of uniting is what Paul elsewhere calls reconciliation.

(b) The uniting of *racial divisions*. In this passage Paul is thinking mainly of Jewish–Gentile relations. This was a crucial divide. He expounds in Chapter 2 how God bridged this gap, but the idea is included in his concise statement here.

(c) *The uniting of all things*. A more difficult concept is next introduced. Paul sees sin as having affected the balance of nature. This thought has something to say on the matter of the environment. Christians must see the creation as a whole as God sees it.

On what grounds unity is possible

For Paul, everything centres in Christ. Since he elsewhere sees Christ as the creator and as the objective of the universe (cf. Col. 1:15ff), he sees everything revolving around Christ.

It is because of Christ's work that reconciliation is attainable.

When such unity was made possible

Paul links it with the *fullness of time*. This expression points to a specially prepared historic moment. God's plans are always precise.

The incarnation–death–resurrection of Christ, seen as one event in history, happened at the most appropriate time.

The coming of Christ brought a binding principle into human affairs.

> *Because of the coming of Christ, it is still the most*
> *appropriate time for divisions to be healed. The*
> *gospel is still the great reconciler.*

EPHESIANS 1:11–14
Our great salvation

In this letter Paul considers the way in which the
gospel came to his readers. He recognises that God
was working out his plans. What he says, however,
is timeless. Salvation never becomes outdated.

Salvation is a provision of God

Here the apostle stresses the importance of God's will and purpose. What God wills he accomplishes. There is never room for failure in the purposes of God. Paul is deeply convinced about the sovereignty of God.

Salvation is universal

(a) Paul first mentions the *Jewish Christians*. This is what he means by 'we who first hoped in Christ'. Of these people he makes two points:

    1. *Their divine assignment.* They were destined and appointed.

    2. *Their objective.* To live for the praise of his glory.

Of course the same points apply equally to the

Gentiles, but Paul is here speaking out of his own experience.

(b) He then includes the *Gentiles*. Note the words 'in whom also you have believed'. It makes no difference that one group was before the other.

All have to hear the word of truth. All have a guaranteed inheritance. Everything is directed to the glory of God.

Salvation is applied by the Spirit

What is meant here by *the seal of the Spirit*? The Spirit indicates ownership. There can be no confusing of identity for the people of God.

The seal is linked with the guarantee. What is true now foreshadows what is to come.

*The gospel has not been left to chance. God
intends that it should belong to those who believe.*

EPHESIANS 1:11, 12
The believer's inheritance

*It is good sometimes to reflect on our future
destiny. We should meditate on what the Christian
may look forward to. Paul helps us here.*

The nature of the inheritance

This includes both the present and the future benefits of the gospel.

The basis of the inheritance

It is exclusively 'in Christ'. There is no other way that people may possess it.

The planning of the inheritance

Every will and testament is planned in advance. God's legacy to man is no exception.

The consequence of the inheritance
The heirs cannot fail to be full of praise to God.

*With such a legacy, how sad that anyone should
miss it through unbelief!*

EPHESIANS 1:13, 14
The sealing of the Spirit

*A seal can be either a mark of ownership, or an
authentication of someone's word. It is an apt
illustration of the Spirit's work in believers.*

The nature of the sealing
It is an accomplished fact. A seal pressed into wax leaves an
impression. We can recognise what was on the seal by the
impression it leaves behind.

The one who seals – God
It is God who anoints us (cf. 2 Cor. 1:22). The sealing must
clearly be done by another.

The one in whom we are sealed – Jesus Christ
God set his seal upon Jesus (Jn. 6:27). This illustrates what
he will do for us for Christ's sake. Those 'in him' receive the
same treatment.

The one who constitutes the seal – the Spirit
The Spirit is the seal and causes his fruit to grow. He
bestows gifts, but most radical of all, he is himself the
greatest gift.

The ones who are sealed
These are clearly believers as verse 13 shows. In the book of
Revelation it is the followers of the lamb who are sealed
(see Rev. 7).

The permanence of the seal
It continues until we acquire possession of the inheritance.
It is a foretaste of what is to come.

*Christians are people with a special stamp upon
them. Not everyone will recognise this, but they
themselves know what security this gives.*

EPHESIANS 1:15–23
A far-reaching prayer

*Paul's prayers are valuable as patterns. They are
also informative about his Christian life and
experience.*

It was informed
Paul knew about the people for whom he was praying. He
knew about their faith. He also knew about their love for
others.

It was thankful
Whenever he remembered he gave thanks. Christian gratitude for what God has done should be continuous. We
never reach the exhaustion point in thanksgiving.

It was based on a right view of God
Paul was praying to the God of our Lord Jesus Christ and
the Father of glory. We note that the thought of glory
dominates this prayer.

It was a request for knowledge
Prayers for further enlightenment must always be relevant.
We never reach saturation point in our understanding of
spiritual truths.

It was a request for glory
Our inheritance is so glorious, we need God's help in
appreciating it.

It was a request for power
In human affairs, power is all too often dangerous. But Paul wants believers to increase in God's power. Indeed he sees that power as incomparably great. But it is God, not man, who controls the power.

It was a desire to know the resurrection
To grasp the extent of the power, we need to consider the significance of the resurrection. Paul saw it as the greatest demonstration of power. It was the shattering of death. It released a similar power for our living.

It was an affirmation
The superiority of Christ is seen in his supremacy over all other agencies. It is also seen in Christ's headship, and further in his filling of all things.

Prayer does not consist exclusively of asking.
Some more important aspects consist in worship,
thanksgiving and affirmation.

EPHESIANS 1:15, 16
Paul's concern for God's people

The apostle was intensely interested in people. His
letters abound in prayers for their spiritual
development.

The true nature of spiritual development
Development cannot be measured in statistics. The most developed churches are not necessarily those with most members.

Paul stresses quality rather than quantity. He speaks of *faith in the Lord* and *love for all the saints*.

Faith and love form part of all Paul's lists of virtues.

The gratitude that such development brings out
Paul has not stopped giving thanks. Nothing rejoices the

hearts of God's servants more than the spiritual development of God's people.

The prayer support that such development demands
Paul assures the readers that he remembers them in his prayers.

He regards praying for others as so natural that he constantly refers to it. No Christian community ever gets to the place of being able to develop without prayer.

Test out your spiritual prosperity on the touchstone of faith and love, and examine whether enough prayer has gone into your development.

EPHESIANS 1:17–19
Spiritual knowledge

Knowledge is of various kinds. But spiritual knowledge differs radically from all forms of natural knowledge. Paul makes this clear in this passage.

The source of spiritual knowledge
   (a) This knowledge comes *from God*.
   (b) It is essentially a *revelation*.
   (c) It is *through the Spirit*.

The channel of spiritual knowledge
It does not come through natural means. But it comes in other ways.
   (a) Through *the eyes of the heart*. This means through the spiritual man's powers of discernment.
   (b) Through *enlightenment*. God gives light that makes spiritual truth intelligible.

The content of spiritual knowledge
   (a) It concerns Christ. It is a particular kind of knowledge.

(b) It concerns the believer's glorious inheritance.

(c) It concerns the power of God. This means it is immeasurably great.

With such a potential for Christian understanding, why should we not grow in knowledge? It is no wonder that Paul speaks of the Christian hope.

EPHESIANS 1:18
The hope of God's call

Hope is a frequently occurring New Testament theme. It is a particular favourite with Paul.

We are called by God through the Spirit
In Ephesians *called* is linked to *election* (cf. 1:5). Throughout God takes the initiative. We simply respond.

Our calling is the basis of our hope
Once we know we are called we can confidently hope for the future.

Our hope is centred in a glorious inheritance
God's giving is always unstinting. Our present blessings are a foretaste of greater to follow.

While the Christian does not live in the future, he knows he has an assured destiny.

EPHESIANS 1:19, 20
Resurrection power

Paul never tires of mentioning the consequences of the resurrection of Christ. It is the mainspring of all Christian action.

The resurrection of Christ is an historical fact
Paul does not discuss this, but he clearly assumes it. Power does not come from a fiction.

The resurrection is a demonstration of a divine power
There is no greater power than that which conquers death. From the time of the earliest Christian preaching the resurrection was seen as an act of God, the supreme example of divine power.

The resurrection supplies believers with power
The same power which raised Christ from the dead is available to us.

With such power at our disposal, why are we so weak?

EPHESIANS 1:19–23
The Father's mighty power

The focus of attention in this prayer is on God's strength rather than on man's weakness. Paul recognises the infinite resources of God.

Power is seen in the miracle of Christ's resurrection
God's power is seen in creation and in the maintenance of the material world. But it is seen supremely in the resurrection of Christ.

Power is seen also in the ascension
The ascension was necessary to restore Christ to his rightful place – at the right hand of God. Christ is therefore now sharing the seat of power. He is superior to all others who aspire to power.

Power is seen in Christ being set over all things
Here is a wide-ranging thought. For everything to be put under his feet means that everything will acknowledge his authority.

Power is seen in the appointment of Christ as head
For Paul, Christ is head over all things for the church, which is more comprehensive than being head of the church. To be concerned for the church involves the whole created order.

There is no lack of power. There is only a failure on our part to comprehend the extent of the power.

EPHESIANS 1:20–23
The superiority of Christ

A Christian's spiritual life will be determined by his view of Christ. It is important therefore to consider how our view of him can be expanded.

His exalted status
(a) *Seated on the right hand of God.* No higher status is available. This is a strong theme in the New Testament (cf. Heb. 1:3; 8:1; also the enthroned Lamb in the book of Revelation).
   The exaltation of Christ is central to his present work. Note that the *right hand* is a position of special privilege.
(b) *Superior to all other authority.* Paul lists some of these – rule, authority, power, dominion. Moreover, Christ's superiority spans both present and future.

His indisputable authority
   (a) *All things are under him.* This is the divine pattern.
       Paul mentions it in 1 Cor. 15:25, although in that case
       he is thinking of a subjection in the future.
   (b) *He is appointed to be head.* The analogy is clear. The
       head is the most important part of the body and
       exercises control over all the members.
   (c) *He is the fullness of the church.* Christ exercises his
       authority through his people.

*This survey of the superiority of Christ shows the
importance Paul attached to a right view of Christ.
It should prompt all Christians to make sure their
view of him is high enough.*

EPHESIANS 1:22, 23
The headship of Christ

*Leadership in all realms is important.
Organisations can rise or fall depending on who is
the head.*

Headship of creation
Paul recognises Christ's part in creation. In Col. 1:15ff.,
he describes Christ as the creator. Here the headship
goes further and focusses on God's purpose for his
church.

Headship of the church
This is different from headship of creation for various
reasons:
   There is an organic oneness.
   Christ has redeemed the church.
   He has a special purpose for his people (cf. 1:15ff.).

Headship involves fullness

The head is so closely linked with the body that the fullness of the head also fills the body. The body becomes charged with divine power and character.

Paul's ideas of the relationship between Christ and his people are both reassuring and challenging. What practical effect does the headship of Christ have on our attitudes and actions?

EPHESIANS 2:1–10
A spiritual history

It is good to make a periodic review of our spiritual pilgrimage. It can be an encouragement. It can also be revealing of our present weakness. Whatever the result, it is a valuable exercise.

The former state

Several features are stressed by way of reminder.

(a) *Spiritually dead.* Sin deludes people into thinking they are alive, when they are not. The natural man is bereft of spiritual life.

(b) *Following the prince of the power of the air.* Paul elsewhere calls our spiritual enemy Satan. He regards all who are not following Christ as being followers of Satan. Such a clear-cut division is not popular, but it cannot be erased from Paul's thought.

(c) *Allied with the disobedient.* The devil's main aim is to get people to disobey.

(d) *Indulging in passions.* People in general follow their desires. This is the world's custom. It is particularly true of the desires of the body. This is especially reflected in our modern permissive society.

(e) *Children of wrath.* Those who are so described are those who deserve God's wrath. This applies naturally to everyone.

39

The transformation

The 'but' of verse 4 marks a dramatic change.

(a) *The change is wrought by God.*

(b) *God has acted out of mercy and love.* Both are described in lavish terms.

(c) *God has brought life out of death.* Believers are made alive with Christ.

(d) *God has raised us with Christ.* Paul is deeply affected by the power of the resurrection.

(e) *God has exalted us with Christ.* Sitting with him means sharing his glory.

So great is this transformation that it shows God's immeasurable grace towards us.

The present position

(a) *We are now saved.* There is a close connection between grace and faith. Neither depends on anything that we can do. Salvation is not by works. God leaves no room for human boasting.

(b) *We are his workmanship.* God rejoiced over the creation of the world. He delights equally in the new creation. He has planned our lives. Good works are the result, not the basis of our salvation.

The change from darkness to light involves a change from the desires of the flesh to the desire for God's ways for us. The two are incompatible.

EPHESIANS 2:1–7
The resurrection and ascension of the believer

In the previous section Paul has brought out the power which results from the resurrection and ascension of Christ. He now sees a parallel in the experience of the believer.

The resurrection of the believer

The believer has been dead in sin. Spiritual corruption had set in. There was no hope apart from a miracle. But when we were in this state God made us alive.

The miracle of Easter becomes the pattern for the spiritual experience of every believer.

The ascension of the believer

Paul recognises the significance of Christ's ascension. He was exalted at the right hand of God.

He sees believers already sitting with Christ. To be 'with him' is to share his victory, i.e. to reign with him.

The consequence

God's riches are seen in his acts of grace towards men. As the resurrection and ascension of Christ demonstrate his power, so his act on behalf of believers shows his grace.

Christians may look forward to discovering more of what Paul calls the immeasurable riches of God's grace.

The resurrection and the ascension have dramatic results for the believer. What is already seen as a historic fact for Christ becomes an ever increasing discovery for himself.

41

EPHESIANS 2:2, 3
The walk of death

*The New Testament often uses the figure of
walking for a person's manner of life. Two kinds
of walk are contrasted here (cf. verses 2 and 10).
The walk of death is paradoxical but real. Paul
speaks here of three powerful influences.*

The world
'The course of this world' means the whole way of life apart
from God. The standards are so different. In the world self
plays a much more dominant part. Christians are expected
to oppose this manner of life.

The devil
Paul calls the devil 'the prince of the power of the air, the
spirit which works in the children of disobedience'. His
influence is adverse, but men are still answerable for their
sins.

The flesh
Paul speaks of the passions of our flesh. This is further
explained as desires of body and mind, i.e. the whole
person. This brings out the self-centred character of the
natural man.

*Only a radical act of God can rescue people from
the walk of death and introduce them to what God
has prepared for them.*

EPHESIANS 2:4–7
The God of our salvation

*In the course of his letters, Paul often gives
incidental insights into the nature of God as he
does here. It is particularly significant when Paul is
writing about God's work of salvation.*

The mercy of God
This is seen in the Old Testament (Mic. 7:18). Paul calls
God the 'Father of mercies' in 2 Cor. 1:3. Note here the
richness of the mercy. Mercy tempers the righteous judgment of God.

The love of God
The greatness of God's love prompted his rescue operation. Love is an integral part of the nature of God. He
cannot act without love.

The grace of God
Grace is God's unmerited favour. It proceeds from love. It
is the basis of our salvation.

The kindness of God
Grace and kindness are closely linked. Kindness brings out
the quality of sympathetic understanding.

*We can never fully fathom the nature of God. We
should be grateful for every new glimpse. We can
never know all there is to know about him.*

EPHESIANS 2:8–10
Salvation

*Paul is setting out here the contrast between faith
and works. It is between accepting what God has
done and relying on our own efforts.*

Salvation is a present reality
Paul speaks of a past act – you have been saved. It has been
experienced only through faith. Indeed the idea of earning
salvation is ruled out. We have it only because God has
given it.

Salvation includes power for good works
Although works cannot earn salvation, they should result
from it. We are his workmanship, created for good works.
  This puts the emphasis on God's design for us.

Salvation is God's provision
This is seen in several particulars – God's grace, God's gift,
God's workmanship, God's preparation. Add to this the
stress on faith.
  Man has no part in this except to accept it.

*Many would have preferred to earn salvation to
provide a sense of achievement. But Paul totally
rejects such a view.*

EPHESIANS 2:11–22
Reconciliation by means of a cross

*The perennial question is 'Why the cross?' Paul
here provides one answer – the reconciliation of
Jew and Gentile. This is an example of the power
of the gospel to heal rifts.*

The problem of separation
Paul emphasises man's plight in a number of ways.
  (a) *Separated from Christ.* This is the condition of the
      natural man. Nevertheless the non-Christian is not
      conscious that such separation exists.
  (b) *Alienated.* Paul is primarily concerned here with
      Gentiles. They were outside the covenant, but are no
      longer so.
  (c) *Strangers.* Under the old covenant Gentiles could
      not belong on the same terms as the Jews. Under the
      new covenant none need be strangers.
  (d) *Without hope and without God.* To be without God is
      the utmost tragedy. Most people do not see it as
      disastrous until things go wrong.
  (e) *Far off.* This suggests a condition of remoteness and
      the absence of communication. This vividly ex-
      presses the true state of the natural man.
  (f) *Hostility.* This denotes more active opposition.
      Apathy often leads ultimately to revolt.
This list emphasises man's need.

The astonishing bridge
It required a miracle to bridge the Jewish–Gentile rift. But
the cross achieved it.
  (a) *Brought near by the blood of the cross.* In some way
      which baffles our understanding the death of Jesus
      overcame the obstacles.
  (b) *The dividing wall broken down.* This is an allusion to
      the dividing curtain in the Temple which was split
      from top to bottom when Jesus died (Matt. 27: 51).

(c) *The law of commandments and ordinances ended.*
Paul's meaning is that God did away with the legal
approach and so opened the way for the Gentiles.

(d) *Hostility brought to an end.* How did God do it? Was
it by overwhelming the alien with love? Or was it by
removing the hostility through Christ? Paul presupposes the latter.

The remarkable results

We may not understand how God works, but we can
experience the results.

(a) *Peace.* Christ is our peace (verse 14). Christ made
peace (verse 15). Christ preached peace (verse 17).

(b) *Access.* Now the Jew and the Gentile share the same
access. There is now no ritual access, nor priests.
Access is aided by the Spirit.

(c) *A new community.* We are fellow citizens. We are
members of God's household. We are a holy temple.

*The reconciliation through the cross is far
reaching. It is still powerful today.*

EPHESIANS 2:11–22
The spiritual temple

*The idea of a material temple for worship is
familiar. But Paul transfers the thought to a
spiritual temple and this introduces some
fascinating truths.*

The kind of material used

Paul is conscious of the characteristics of the Gentile
Christians. They have a history of spiritual deficiency. He
describes their state in verses 11, 12.

But the making of Jew and Gentile into one new creature
provides new possibilities for a true spiritual temple – one
based on spiritual values.

The foundation
Here Paul is thinking of the apostolic witness as the foundation. Elsewhere it is Christ (1 Cor. 3:11).

There is no real difference since the apostles bore witness to Christ.

The corner stone
This is a different illustration from that in 1 Cor. 3. The corner stone binds the walls together.

Both Jew and Gentile need to depend on Christ. It is this common factor which is a strong bond.

The unity
Paul recognises the extraordinary nature of the Christian gospel in bringing Jew and Gentiles into harmony.

The same principle can overcome all divisions, whether racial, social or intellectual. Christ is the great uniter.

The one who dwells within
This is the Spirit. The nature of the temple is determined by its occupant. Paul sees a spiritual temple, because the Spirit dwells within. This is how he can speak of its growth.

Since the Spirit occupies the temple it is not surprising that Paul calls it 'holy'.

Since all believers are part of this spiritual temple, it must have some dramatic practical effects. Both individually and corporately Christians must act in a way that is worthy of the indwelling Spirit.

EPHESIANS 2:11–13
Change of status

*Contrasts are often useful when we are evaluating
our experiences. It is good to make such
comparisons in the spiritual realm, as Paul does
here.*

Remember what you were

We should not dwell in the past, but some recollection is
valuable. To recall what we were enables us to appreciate
what we are now.

The Gentiles were aliens, away from God. Alienation is
the state of the natural man.

Remember what you are

The 'but now' of verse 13 has a greater force when seen
against the former state. A remarkable change has been
effected in Christ.

Since our Christian spiritual experiences are all through
Christ, memory of the past should enhance our view of him.

*We are called on to live in the present, but not to
neglect the lessons from the past.*

EPHESIANS 2:12
Those far from God

*Paul is concerned not only with those blatantly far
off, who have no time for God or are actively
opposed to him, but with all who are outside the
covenant. In fact he regards all who are not 'in
Christ' as being 'far off'.*

They are distinguished from God's people

Paul thinks primarily of the Gentiles, who were uncircum-
cised. He sees their position as more alienated than that of

the Jews. Nevertheless both need to come to God through Christ. Faith in Christ becomes more important than any external rite, like circumcision.

They are aliens
An alien is a person who does not belong. The commonwealth of Israel has now become expanded to include all peoples. Note the reference to 'fellow citizens' in verse 19.

They are strangers
Those 'far off' have no natural opportunity to gain acquaintance with God. But in Christ they can draw near on equal terms. The stranger can become a member of the family of God.

They are without hope
They may not recognise this condition. But all without God are ultimately without hope. What was generally true of the Gentile world is reflected in all who attempt to live apart from God.

To be brought near to God was the greatest experience for these people. It still is for us.

EPHESIANS 2:13–18
Christ our peace

Everyone has a desire for peace. But what kind of peace? Paul is here discussing spiritual peace. This is the kind which consists of inward harmony.

Our peace proceeds from Christ
Paul can identify Christ and peace. Our notion of peace must be controlled by his nature.

His incarnation heralded peace (Luke 2:14). He promised peace to his disciples (John 14:27).

The Christian cannot divorce peace from Christ. Christ has removed the dividing wall of hostility which separated man from God.

Christ makes peace

This has been true historically. Racial barriers were done away with. The formidable Jewish–Gentile feud was offered a workable solution.

There are no divisions which Christ cannot bridge. Consider Paul's statement in Gal. 3:28.

Christ proclaims peace

Peace sums up the mission of Christ. It sums up reconciliation. Christ's death and resurrection removed the obstacles.

All men (Jew and Gentile alike) now have access
to God. Racial equality is one of the most far
reaching blessings of the gospel.

EPHESIANS 2:18
Access to the Father

Man's most pressing quest is how to approach
God.

We come to God as to a father

This is the supreme revelation of God which Jesus brought. This is a concept which we can understand.

We come to him through Christ.

The words 'through him' point to Christ as high priest, as forerunner. Christ has opened up a new and living way (cf. Heb. 10:20).

We come to him in the Spirit

Since it is through the Spirit we are born again, we are in the Spirit when we come to God.

Here we have the Trinity involved in enabling us to
communicate with God.

EPHESIANS 2:19
Fellow citizens

*The idea of the church as a city is familiar in the
New Testament. It is seen especially in the idea of
the New Jerusalem (Heb. 12:22; Rev. 21 and 22).*

The city idea points to stability
Cities are built as corporate communities. The group is as
important as the individual.

The Gentiles have become citizens
Previously they were strangers. They possessed no citizen
rights. They had been spiritually homeless, but they had
now become full members of the people of God.

Citizens have special responsibilities
They are described as saints. This means their conduct must
conform to a high standard. The household of God exists to
please God.

*It should be a matter of pride to be a citizen of a
city whose builder and maker is God (cf. Heb.
11:10).*

EPHESIANS 2:20–22
The church as the temple of God

*The temple illustration follows on from the idea of
a city and of a household. The focus shifts here to a
worship idea.*

The stable foundation
These were the apostles and prophets. From a human point
of view the apostles founded the church (as Acts shows).

51

But they testified to Christ, who is the real foundation.

When Paul calls Christ the corner stone it is his way of saying that Christ holds everything together.

The close-knit design

No architect thinks in terms of disparate parts, but in total concepts. No one part can fulfil its function except in relation to the whole.

The whole structure is intended to be joined together.

The importance of growth

Paul does not conceive of a static building. In some sense the building idea proves inadequate, for Paul introduces the concept of growth. The church does not become a holy temple instantaneously.

Paul allows for development, and this should be a constant challenge to God's people. In other language Paul talks similarly of sanctification.

The purpose of the building

It is to be God's dwelling place. This provides for a constant challenge.

Where the Spirit dwells must be in process towards greater holiness.

EPHESIANS 3:1–13
Serving the gospel

This passage draws attention to both the hardships and the joys of being a servant of the gospel. There could be no better example of this than the experience of the apostle.

Suffering for the gospel is seen to be vicarious

Paul is a prisoner on behalf of others.

(a) *His sufferings were intense.* Compare 2 Cor. 11 for a partial list. Even this is quite formidable. Paul's

aim to preach the gospel overcame many obstacles.
   (b) *His sufferings were voluntary.* They were not the
       result of accidents or of unavoidable calamities. He
       embraced hardship for the cause of Christ.
   (c) *His sufferings were Christ-like.* He was deeply con-
       scious of what Christ had endured and saw this as
       something of a pattern.

Revelation is seen to be essential for the gospel

Paul never regarded the gospel as his own discovery. What
insights he had had been given to him. Paul makes three
statements about the mystery.
   (a) *It had been hidden.* The coming of Christ was a
       turning point.
   (b) *It was comprehensive.* The inclusion of Gentiles
       meant the exclusion of no one.
   (c) *It was planned.* Before creation it was in the mind of
       God. Such a gospel is not a passing phase.
The greater the grasp of the greatness of the gospel, the
greater will be the determination to spread it.

The preacher is seen to be God's minister

What Paul says of himself is applicable to all who preach the
gospel.
   (a) *God had appointed him.* Paul sees his ministry as a
       gift. He was under God's orders in his ministry.
   (b) *He showed a true spirit of humility.* The words 'less
       than the least' vividly express this.
   (c) *He grasped the greatness of the gospel.* It was nothing
       less than the unsearchable riches of Christ.
   (d) *He knew his task was to bring light to others.* He
       aimed to make all men see God's plan.
   (e) *He acquired in Christ great boldness.* He rejected a
       fearful or apologetic approach. He knew he had
       access to all the resources of God.

*If we were to take Paul's approach as our example
in the spreading of the gospel, we would discover a
new dynamic.*

EPHESIANS 3:1–13
The apostle to the Gentiles

Paul is here explaining something of his approach to his high calling, especially his mission to the Gentiles.

Paul's relationship to his readers
He describes himself as a prisoner for Jesus Christ. This conjures up all his sufferings in the course of his work. To be a prisoner was not a new experience (cf. 2 Cor. 11:23).

Paul recognises that he suffered on behalf of others, including his readers.

His apostleship was God's appointment
Paul speaks of the stewardship of God's grace. He was given a great responsibility – but he was able to call on God's resources.

His apostleship was linked to the mystery
The mystery had been made known through revelation. Paul is conscious of God's special revelation which he received at his conversion. The mystery here is God's plan for the Gentiles.

He was filled with a sense of unworthiness
Was he exaggerating when he called himself the least of all the saints? Not in the light of his former persecuting zeal. His awareness of what he owed to God's grace never flagged.

His aim was to explain the mystery to others
To make men see it was no easy task, in spite of the fact that the mystery was no longer hidden. It is no easier now to persuade people of the truth of the gospel.

His labours were of interest to the spiritual powers
The gospel meant the death blow to Satanic powers. No wonder they were concerned over its proclamation.

His experience of Christ explains his boldness
Boldness, confidence, not losing heart, were Paul's watch-

words. He found an enormous increase in courage in Christ.

We should marvel at the example of Paul. That example has proved an inspiration to countless Christians. It can still be so for us.

EPHESIANS 3:1
A prisoner of Jesus Christ

Paul was a prisoner when he wrote many of his letters. It was a time of adversity and intense physical discomfort. Paul's approach to his imprisonment provides an inspiration to us still.

He sees imprisonment as part of his Christian service

He does not complain. He actually sees himself as a prisoner belonging to Christ. This is more significant than being a prisoner for Christ's sake, although he certainly was that. He is content to suffer for Christ.

His imprisonment is on behalf of others

Note the words 'for the sake of you Gentiles'. Conscious of being the apostle to the Gentiles, Paul regards his sufferings as necessary for the accomplishment of his mission.

The reason for the imprisonment greatly affects the attitude of the prisoner. What he suffers is for Christ and for others.

He regards his imprisonment as an influence for good

It gave him an opportunity to write. This and other priceless letters grew out of his imprisonment. These letters have provided rich teaching for the Christian church ever since.

The profoundness of Paul's thought is due in no small measure to his triumph over hardship.

Many are still in prison for Christ's sake. Several gems of literature have emerged from prisons (e.g.

Pilgrim's Progress). Those at present in prison for Christ deserve the special support of God's people.

EPHESIANS 3:2–6
God's plan for the Gentiles

In Paul's day the Jews regarded the Gentiles as outside the covenant. They were the religiously underprivileged. But Paul has come to a larger understanding of God's plan for them.

God's plan proceeded from his grace
Paul has experienced that grace. He sees it as part of an extensive plan.

That plan, once a mystery, is now known
Other generations had no knowledge of it. But the Spirit has now revealed it.

Paul has provided an exposition of it
It was made known to him by revelation. His readers could now follow his insights.

The plan moulds Jews and Gentiles into a unity
They are heirs together, members together, sharers together. God's plans are not divisive.

The merging of Jew and Gentile required a powerful agency. If God could do this for the Gentiles, he can overcome all barriers.

EPHESIANS 3:4–6
Insight

Many think that the gospel is unintelligible. It is, if approached solely from the point of view of human reason. Paul recognised the need for an additional factor, i.e. God-given insight.

Others could perceive it
Paul is certain his readers should be able to do this. What did he mean? He evidently thought that a true understanding of the gospel should be transparent.

It was not known to previous generations
Paul is no doubt thinking of the pre-Christian age. Some hints of the mystery were given during this period. But the main revelation had not happened, for Christ had not come. The lack of insight was therefore understandable.

It is now given to the apostles
Paul knows he has received it. But he is not alone. The apostles and prophets have also received it. It is the age of the Spirit.

It has led to a marvellous revelation
The rift between Jew and Gentile has been healed. This was nothing but a miracle. They are now fellow heirs, fellow members of the same body, fellow partakers of the same promise.

The insight that the gospel is universal has overcome all national and racial barriers. It is a challenge in a world still racked by racial tensions. Modern Christians must demonstrate it in practice.

EPHESIANS 3:8
Less than the least

*One's image of oneself is of great importance.
Some think too much of themselves; some too
little. Surely here Paul is underrating himself? But
his idea of himself is against the background of
God's grace.*

Paul's high view of grace led to a low view of self
Grace is God's free favour towards man. Paul saw the
whole gospel as evidence of God's grace. By comparison he
recognised his own resources as negligible.

His low view of self proved valuable in God's service
God uses those who depend least upon themselves.
Preaching the gospel demands a high degree of dependence
on God's grace.

*We need not be afraid of a low view of ourselves if
it leads to a more effective use of God's power.*

EPHESIANS 3:12
Christian boldness

*People naturally vary in the degree of boldness
they possess. It is so often a matter of
temperament. But when it comes to Christian
witness different conditions apply. The naturally
timid may become incredibly bold before God.*

Boldness is exercised in approaching God
This is where the believer learns to develop confidence.
Initially there is overwhelming awe. But this gives way to
boldness since God has provided the access. Yet however
bold we become, we must still draw near with reverence.

Boldness is based on our relationship to Christ

It is only through him that we can confidently come (Heb. 10:19ff.).

We are not accepted on our own merits. Christian boldness is therefore totally different from self-confidence. We know that it is only through Christ that we are reconciled to God.

Boldness is possible only through faith

If we relied on good works, we could never come with assurance. Paul rejects justification through works.

Faith consists in accepting what God has provided.

Christians are called on to approach God not in terror, but with confidence.

EPHESIANS 3:14–21
Prayer for enrichment

This is another of Paul's prayers which will repay careful study. We may consider how far it reflects the kind of prayers we pray.

Introduction

(a) The *attitude* of the petitioner – I bow my knees.
(b) The *character* of the one approached – the Father.
(c) The *subjects* of the prayer – members of God's family.

The petitions

(a) The *nature* of the prayer – for strengthening.
(b) The *measure* for the requests – the riches of God's glory.
(c) The *specific* requests – for indwelling, stability, understanding, knowledge, fullness.

Doxology

(a) The *praise* of God. Here it is specially because of his power.

(b) The *glory* of God. This is seen in both Christ and his church.

(c) The *duration*. It is for ever and ever.

Such a prayer never loses its relevance. Christians never reach the point of not needing it.

EPHESIANS 3:14–19
A prayer for others

Although personal prayer is a vital part of Christian living, it is prayer for others which is most enriching.

The one who prays
Paul bows the knee, the posture of humility.

The one addressed
God as Father. This family illustration introduces intimacy.

The expectation
The target is no less a standard than the riches of God's glory.

The requests
Paul concentrates on spiritual blessings – strength, stability, love, understanding.

The climax is reached in the prayer for God's fullness. It is impossible to conceive of a nobler prayer than this.

EPHESIANS 3:16–19
Prayer with a large vision

Paul's letters are full of prayers. Their main characteristic is their breadth of vision. They provide a challenging pattern. In this one there is a five-fold prayer.

For strength for the inward man

This is for inward strength, i.e. spiritual and moral. We often survive on minimum spiritual energy. Paul does not encourage inertia or apathy.

He sees strength as:
God's gift,
the Spirit's supply, and
measured only by God's riches.

For the indwelling of Christ

Paul knows that Christ dwells in all Christians. Why then the prayer? He wants them to have an increasing awareness of the indwelling Christ. In what sense does the Christ within control our desires?

For a firm basis in love

Paul uses an agricultural metaphor. Roots are vital for plant growth. The roots extract the goodness from the soil. Love is here seen as a kind of spiritual compost.

Paul also uses an architectural metaphor. Buildings depend on good foundations. Love is a wonderful basis for the Christian life – cf. 1 Cor. 13.

For an increasing understanding of Christ's love

Paul switches from human love to Christ's love. There is need for enabling – an understanding wholly beyond man's natural capacity.

Love is presented here in spatial terms. This is to demonstrate its vastness. Paul is in fact praying that the Christians might know the unknowable.

For an infilling of the fullness of God

This seems an impossible prayer (cf. Col. 1:19), which

61

speaks of all God's fullness dwelling in Christ. Paul's use of 'all' here is specially surprising. This is an ultimate aim. Paul sets his sights at the highest level.

This series of petitions builds up into an impressive prayer. Does it show up the poverty and narrowness of our prayers?

EPHESIANS 3:18, 19
The dimensions of love

Paul is here attempting to describe the indescribable.

Love is seen to be limitless
Spatial dimensions here point to the impossibility of defining the boundaries. Where are the fences beyond which love is prohibited?

Yet love can be the object of knowledge
At least it can be when Christ's love is involved. Knowing his love is a progressive experience. Love will, nevertheless, always surpass knowledge.

Love reaches its expression in God's fullness
To have the fullness of God means to have the fullness of his love. This is love of the noblest kind.

No one can suppose that he has fully attained this kind of love.

EPHESIANS 3:20, 21
Doxology

Paul's doxologies are always worth pondering.

The subject
It is God who works powerfully within us. His power exceeds our wildest dreams.

The sphere
God's glory is seen in the church and in Christ. There would be no church apart from Christ. There is no other sphere in which God is so gloriously seen.

The duration
To all generations, for ever and ever. God's glory will outlast all time.

We could not do better than to make this doxology our own.

EPHESIANS 4:1–16
The unity of the church

The first part of this section deals with the Christian's calling. It contains a direct appeal from a Christian prisoner. It is based on experience – even imprisonment for Christ. It is a challenge which cannot be ignored.

Paul points out:
   (a) God sets his own standards.
   (b) This involves new attitudes.
   (c) This must lead to unity.
It requires effort and the Spirit's help.

The unifying facts
Paul sets out Christian unity in a sevenfold form.
- (a) *One body*. All have the same head.
- (b) *One Spirit*. Each part is indwelt by the same Spirit.
- (c) *One hope*. All Christians are heirs to the same promises.
- (d) *One Lord*. All must confess Christ as Lord.
- (e) *One faith*. All the members have become so through faith.
- (f) *One baptism*. All are baptised in the name of Jesus – no other baptism is valid.
- (g) *One God and Father*. All believers can say 'Our Father'.

Division and disunity are clearly alien to these facts.

The unifying gifts
Christians are people of grace, which is essentially undeserved. The idea here is of a conqueror bestowing gifts. Christ first had to ascend before giving the gifts. The gifts here are different offices for the church.
- (a) *Apostles*. These were specially commissioned to witness to the resurrection.
- (b) *Prophets*. Those with the gift of prophecy would give messages from God.
- (c) *Evangelists*. These would proclaim the good news to needy people.
- (d) *Pastors and teachers*. These would tend and instruct the church.

What are these offices for?
  The equipping of Christians,
  the ministering to others,
  the building up of the church.

The unifying developments
The results are not in doubt.
- (a) All are to *attain* to unity, knowledge and maturity.
- (b) All are to *avoid* vacillation. They are to avoid being like unpredictable children, flotsam or litter.
- (c) All are to *grow up*. How? By speaking the truth in love, growing up into the head (Christ), being knit

together with others – like joints depending on other joints for a proper functioning.

We must ask ourselves the question – what are we doing to foster Christian unity?

EPHESIANS 4:1–6
The Christian life

Paul thinks of the Christian life as a walk.

A persuasive plea
He uses a strong word of exhortation as if some moral pressure was required. Certainly he sees himself as a pattern.

A fixed quality
The Christian has a calling and his walk must be worthy of it. He cannot fix his own standards.

A social responsibility
The qualities mentioned – lowliness, meekness, forbearance – are all passive virtues which promote harmony with others. It is love which binds them all together.

A spiritual unity
Christians are not isolated individuals – they are bound together by the same unity. Such a bond must be a bond of peace. Paul illustrates this unity in a sevenfold way.

In this section Paul sets out a high pattern for Christian living.

EPHESIANS 4:3–6
Basic Christian unities

Paul has no doubt about the importance of unity.
His reflections on the theme are intensely practical.

All belong to one organism
The body is not an organisation but a living organism.

All are indwelt by one Spirit
Elsewhere Paul is clear that all who acknowledge Christ do so through the Spirit. This is the only way.

All share one inheritance
Our hope is centred in a heavenly inheritance. God makes no distinctions in his promises to believers.

All serve one Lord
Acknowledging Christ as Lord and Master puts all on the same footing.

All have one faith
Salvation is received by faith. But faith here may stand for the comprehensive Christian position.

All have one baptism
All Christians are baptised into Christ.

All worship one God
It is basic to Christian revelation that there is one God. This distinguishes it from polytheism and also atheism. Our God is known as Father.

Wherever attention is paid to these unities there are
strong bonds of fellowship.

EPHESIANS 4:7–16
The gift of Christ

Here Paul speaks of both the gift (grace) and the gifts (ministries). He sees them as inextricably bound together.

The gift is given by Christ

Whenever Paul speaks of grace, it is always as a gift. Here is a reminder that no one can boast in his own achievements. The gospel is essentially God's gift to us.

The gift is the result of what Christ has done

Paul reflects on the incarnation (descent) and the ascension of Christ – the two events which encompass the historic work of Christ on earth. God's gift to us is the direct result of Christ's finished work.

The gift is channelled through a variety of ministries

The one gift comes through many agents. Clearly not all have the same function, but all have received the function they have.

The gift has the purpose of building up the church

The variety of ministries are for:
> equipping the church,
> bringing about unity and maturity,
> developing stability in place of vacillation,
> knitting Christians together in love.

When Christ gives gifts they are not for selfish purposes, but for the noblest possible ends.

EPHESIANS 4:8–10
The importance of the ascension

Paul's concern here is with the ascension, which presupposes the fact of the resurrection.

It is seen in terms of a conqueror's triumph
The exaltation of Christ is seen through Ps. 68:18.

The leading of captives in a triumphal procession demonstrates Christ's victory over the powers of darkness. The gifts are given to those who witness the victory.

It is seen to have a positive effect for the church
The different offices necessary for the development of the church are seen to be Christ's appointments.

The ascension was the beginning, not the end of Christ's activity on behalf of his people.

It established the supremacy of Christ
It has enabled him to fill everything. His work and influence are much more expansive now than in his earthly ministry.

The ascension is important because it focusses on the exaltation and present ministry of Christ.

EPHESIANS 4:13–16
Personal maturity

It should be the aim of all Christians to become better Christians. This is the path to maturity. Even if we never fully achieve it, the goal is essential.

The inward growth of the person
Paul speaks of 'mature manhood'. He thinks of the blossoming out of the new person in Christ. He sees this expressed in

knowledge,
stability,
reliability,
love.

The corporate growth of the church

If the individual members reach maturity, the whole body benefits. Growing into Christ, the head, is a corporate activity.

The joints are intimately joined together. If one malfunctions the whole is affected. True growth binds each part together. The growth metaphor demonstrates the interdependence of each.

Maturity can be achieved only by personal discipline and concerted action. Both are equally needed.

EPHESIANS 4:17–24
Moral madness and its antidote

Christianity grew up in an immoral environment. In the Christian era the tension between good and evil continued. Modern sophistication has not changed the situation. Paul uses contemporary Gentile life to illustrate the transforming power of the gospel.

Moral madness

(a) *Darkened understanding.* Paul begins with mental attitudes. The modern world bursts with intelligence, but we need to ask the question whether man's wisdom is enlightened.

In view of nuclear armaments, it must be seriously questioned. So much intelligence leaves out moral values.

(b) *Alienation from God.* This shows the consequences of a darkened understanding. It suggests an attitude of godless self-sufficiency. It develops into a position in opposition to religious thought.

In a godless society, alienation from God is not recognised. Man is content with his own ignorance.

(c) *Hardness of heart.* Hardness destroys sensitivity and produces a lack of recognition of sin, injustice and cruelty. Man easily convinces himself that the end justifies the means.

The conscience becomes encased in a hard shell.

(d) *Licentiousness and greed.* Paul says they have given themselves up to these things. They have capitulated to immorality and materialism. Much modern society is a replica of this.

The antidote

Paul at once identifies it as the Christian position. 'You did not so learn Christ' he comments. A transformation of attitude is required.

(a) *Christian morality has to be learned.* We do not slide into right thinking. Spiritual development involves a process of spiritual education. Paul sums it up as 'learning Christ'.

(b) *We need the right teacher.* Christ is not only the subject, but also the instructor. Our understanding is found in him. This is totally different from the natural approach to morality, which is generally self-centred rather than Christ-centred.

(c) *We need renunciation.* The Christian is called to put off what belongs to the old nature. A radical change of approach is expected. Renunciation is a continuous process.

(d) *We need renewal.* This is the positive side – a new kind of outlook and new standards of judgment. It is the mind which needs renewing because a person acts as he thinks. There must always be a putting on whenever there is a putting off. The new nature is God's creation, not man's.

With such a marvellous provision for us, why do we stick to anything belonging to the old nature?

EPHESIANS 4:17–19
How not to live

*Paul writes to Christians who could remember
their past environment. His description of pagan
life can be regarded as a warning to all.*

Intellect without light

It is central to Paul's view that Christians have renewed and
enlightened minds.

There is a marked distinction from the previous state. It
is not a matter of intellect, but the ability to make moral
judgments. Brilliant minds can be utterly dark over moral
issues.

Life without God

This does not mean that God is absent, but that he is
ignored. The very idea of God becomes alien. He does not
figure in man's calculations. The creature is setting himself
against his creator.

Hearts without sensitivity

A hardening of heart means inability to react to situations
in a selfless way. Finer and nobler considerations are
excluded.

Actions without purity

There is an abandonment to sensuality. Self-indulgence
becomes the norm. Lust is never satisfied.

*Against this analysis of an environment without
God, the superiority of the Christian way becomes
vividly clear. We need sometimes to think
negatively in order to develop more positively.*

EPHESIANS 4:25–32
Things to avoid

*When Paul deals with ethical issues, he rarely
writes in the abstract. He illustrates his points in
practical ways. The samples he selects form a basis
for wider application.*

Falsehood
Truth is an essential Christian virtue. Its opposite must be
rejected. Christians can never have a relative approach to
truth. Their words must always be dependable. They must
always consider others and avoid deceit.

Anger
There is a right type of anger, but most anger is wrong. Paul
urges that anger should be limited to the day of eruption. It
must not be carried forward. It is disastrous to awake with
last night's anger still festering. Paul knows the devil uses
anger as a weapon.

Theft
It seems elementary that a Christian should not steal. But
modern society is riddled with dishonesty and Christians
must beware lest they are also enmeshed. Honest toil is
more satisfying than ill-gotten gains.

Unwholesome speech
Words can become as corrupt as rotten fruit or vegetables.
It is not here so much a question of violent or profane
talk, as words which are not palatable. The positive side
is talk which edifies, which can be a fit channel of grace.
Any talk which detracts rather than builds up must be
avoided.

Rancour
Paul includes a list of vices, all expressing attitudes which
do not enhance the Christian. Indeed, his list of vices is at
once off-set by a list of virtues. The two lists are mutually

exclusive. Bitterness and kindness, anger and forgiveness simply cannot coexist.

Paul slips in a warning about grieving the Spirit which sums up the whole section. It is the Spirit's desire that we avoid these vices. To fail to do so is to grieve him.

EPHESIANS 4:26, 27
Anger

Anger is usually thought of in terms of an outburst of wrath. It is generally regarded as uncontrolled. Yet there is a valid place for anger of the right sort and it is this that Paul deals with here.

Anger need not be sinful
Where anger springs from self-assertion it is wrong, for it is evidence of lack of self control. But some anger can be morally justified (cf. Mark 3:5).

To avoid sinful anger requires effort
Paul sees the need to issue a challenge. It is difficult to be angry and yet not sin, for we must first examine our motives before allowing our anger to rise. Righteous anger cannot be spontaneous.

Anger must not be allowed to continue
Paul suggests that a day is the limit. The sun which marks a new day must not be a witness to yesterday's outburst. Dragged over anger is inappropriate for a new day.

Anger can provide Satan with a foothold
To nurture anger does the devil's work for him. Once it is allowed to fester it is difficult to stop.

Give sufficient thought to anger and it will never get out of control.

EPHESIANS 4:29
Speech

*Christians must watch the way they talk. Speech is
an indication of a way of life. Paul here comments
on speech both negatively and positively.*

The negative aspect

Evil talk is banned. It has no place for the Christian, since in
Christ he has been delivered from evil.

Evil talk debases a valuable God-given gift. It means that
speech is being used to communicate ideas which are alien
to God.

The positive aspect

Speech which is good for edifying builds up others. It is
speech that does not drag down. It conveys God's truth.

Such speech is fitting. It does not degrade any occasion.
It does not spoil what is good. Such speech imparts grace,
which may refer to its manner or to its content. Since the
gospel is gracious, it cannot truly be conveyed in a manner
alien to it.

*Listen to your words.
What function are they performing?
Are they building up the listeners?*

EPHESIANS 4:30
Grieving the Spirit

An exhortation not to grieve the Spirit shows the possibility of it. The statement tells us certain things about the Spirit.

The Spirit is seen as a person
The personality of the Spirit is a powerful truth. The indwelling Spirit is not just an influence or a power at our disposal. He is an honoured guest.

The Spirit is susceptible to grief
This brings out the sensitive nature of the Spirit. Recognition of this should make us more careful to avoid such grieving.

The Spirit has an important role in redemption
Paul gives a reason for his exhortation – because the Spirit has sealed us for the day of our redemption.

Those sealed by the Spirit have an obligation not to grieve him. Christians should develop a sensitivity in this direction.

EPHESIANS 4:31, 32
Wrong and right attitudes

Contrasts are useful in examining attitudes. Paul uses them here to set out what to avoid and what to embrace.

Wrong attitudes
(a) *Bitterness*. Harsh thoughts which lead to sourness.
(b) *Wrath*. The settled attitude of opposition.
(c) *Anger*. The spontaneous outburst.

(d) *Slander*. The spreading of untrue or harmful reports.
(e) *Malice*. The deliberate intent to hurt other people.

Right attitudes
(a) *Kindness*. The opposite of bitterness. The ability to think the best instead of the worst.
(b) *Tenderness*. An openness to the needs of others and an ability to feel with them.
(c) *Forgiveness*. Avoiding harbouring a grudge against anyone. An example is God forgiving us in Christ.

It is not difficult to choose which list is preferable.
Yet it is all too easy to fall into wrong attitudes.

EPHESIANS 5:1–14
How to survive in an adverse environment

This passage deals with the Christian's manner of life. The main emphasis is positive, but as so often Paul pinpoints also the negative side.

A wonderful example
Why should we imitate God? Only because of what he has done in Christ.

Christ loved. He gave himself for us. He is a fragrant offering to God. All this shows the powerful example of love. The Christian has a totally worthy pattern.

A stern warning of wrath
Immorality, covetousness, filthy talk, frivolity – these are the very opposite to God's pattern. These things merit God's wrath. They exclude the perpetrators from the kingdom.

Yet these things were and still are a part of the environment. The Christian cannot walk according to the social custom. He must constantly challenge his environment.

Light must be dissociated from darkness

There must be a marked distinction between them. Association here means condoning darkness. But separation is essential if purity is to be preserved.

Once a person is in the light, it is gross madness to fumble around in the dark. Children of light cannot continue to walk in darkness.

Light is fruitful, whereas darkness is unfruitful

Paul thinks of fruitfulness as producing virtues pleasing to God. The right kind of fruit is good and right and true. But darkness can only produce things it is shameful even to speak of.

Paul is here presenting his case in black and white. What is not light is darkness. He urges his readers to wake up to the light.

The Christian life is meant to be lived in the full glare of light. Christians should have nothing to hide of which they are ashamed. They are children of light.

EPHESIANS 5:1, 2
Imitating God

It is important to have standards. If they are low, behaviour will rise no higher. But here Paul appears to be presenting the impossible.

The command to imitate

This is not an option. It is not reserved for the elite. It is not the standard for super Christians, but for everyone. If we consider God's actions, we shall see our own in their true light.

The reason for imitating

It is because we are 'beloved children'. In a well ordered family, the parents are examples for the children to follow.

God so loves us that our response should be the desire to be like him.

A parallel pattern

To imitate God means to walk in love. Christ's love for us in giving himself is a perfect example. The result is fragrance in God's sight. Here is a reminder that imitating God involves cost.

We need to enquire whether our standards are high enough. Are we afraid of the impossible?

EPHESIANS 5:3–7
Covetousness

This is one of the prohibitions in the Ten Commandments. Jesus named it as one of the evils which defile a person (Mark 7:22). Paul more than once condemns it (1 Cor. 5:10, 11; Rom. 1:29). He makes three points about it.

It is classed with serious sins

Immorality is uncleanness of a sexual nature. Impurity is more general and can include thoughts and speech as well as acts. Covetousness is evil in relation to material possessions.

Paul's classification is startling. Many whose sexual behaviour is pure are nonetheless guilty of covetousness. Are these sins really on the same footing? Paul explains covetousness as idolatry, i.e. worshipping what belongs to others.

It excludes from the kingdom

This is intended to challenge. The kingdom consists of those devoted to the King, not to their own advancement.

Covetousness is as much out of place in the kingdom as immorality.

It attracts God's wrath
It is because of these evils that God's wrath comes on the children of disobedience. Covetousness is one of these evils.

It is opposed to God's will and must therefore merit his wrath.

In view of the seriousness of this sin, the only course of action is to dissociate ourselves firmly from it. But this requires constant vigilance.

EPHESIANS 5:4
Inappropriate speech

Paul is always sensitive about what is fitting, and recognises how vital it is in the sphere of speech.

Varieties of unedifying speech
   (a) *Filthiness*. This refers to obscene or blasphemous speech.
   (b) *Silly talk*. This is talk which centres on foolishness and sin (cf. Matt. 12:36).
   (c) *Levity*. Paul is not here condemning healthy jesting, but words which are allied to lewdness.
The Christian has to learn more acceptable standards.

The inappropriateness of such speech
Paul does not supply reasons, but he assumes that his readers will see how ill-fitting such speech is for the followers of Christ. It is fitting that Christian lips should be seen to be pure.

Such speech should give place to thanksgiving
If the Christian were constantly in an attitude of praise, there would be no time for wrong speech.

Since others notice the way we talk, it is imperative for us continually to guard our lips.

EPHESIANS 5:8–10
Essential changes for Christians

The Christian life calls for radical reappraisals. It is one of its glories that it possesses the secret of change.

Transformation

Once we were in darkness, but now we are in light. No change can be more dramatic. Light cannot tolerate darkness. It shatters it. There is real value in calling to mind our transformation in Christ.

Obligation

We are to walk as children of light. Once having experienced light, it would be unthinkable to continue in darkness. Christians must learn to please the Lord.

Demonstration

We are to bring forth fruit. Fruit trees need light to grow. Similarly the fruit of the Spirit can only flourish in the light. Darkness is essentially unfruitful.

Christian life is never intended to be static. We can never feel that we have arrived. We need constant reminders of what God intends us to be.

EPHESIANS 5:11–14
Two contrasting worlds

People live in different worlds. It is important for Christians to recognise that their world is quite different from that of their contemporaries.

The world of darkness

(a) *Unproductive.* Looked at through Christian eyes the works of the world are described as unfruitful.

(b) *Secretive*. Much dishonest practice is done in secret. What is not seen is often assumed to be legitimate.

(c) *Shameful*. All sin is shameful. But much of the world does not recognise this. Modern pornography is a striking example of this.

(d) *Complacent*. Devotees of darkness need to be aroused from their stupor.

(e) *Spiritually dead*. Darkness and death are closely linked together.

The world of light

What attitude is desirable in such an environment?

(a) *Separation*. Paul urges no association. The children of light do not belong to the works of darkness. But some resolution is needed to maintain this separation.

(b) *Exposure*. This requires more than a passive attitude. It requires courage to expose evil.

(c) *Illumination*. When a light is held up in a dark place, the evils become visible.

(d) *Challenge*. We must not allow our environment to have a soporific effect on us. We must arouse those around us.

Since Christians have discovered the light, they have a responsibility to make it known to others.

EPHESIANS 5:14
The call of the gospel

This may have been an extract from a Christian hymn. It sums up the challenge of the gospel.

To whom it is addressed

The sleeper. Some think this is addressed to a community which needs more action. Others take it as words addressed to non-Christians, i.e. the spiritually dead.

Sleep is a good metaphor for the unregenerate. The gospel calls people to awake from their dead state. They are dead in trespasses and in sins.

The nature of the command
How can a dead person awake? Clearly not through any power of his own. It is the genius of the gospel to give power to those who are dead in sins to enable them to respond to it. It awakens a recognition of need.

The promise to those who respond
The needy must realise the darkness. But they must also assume that light exists, if their state is to be improved. Such light is attainable only through Christ. Jesus himself claimed to be the light of the world (John 8:12).

Every preacher of the gospel is echoing God's call as it is expressed in this passage.

EPHESIANS 5:15–20
The walk of the wise

Paul's view of wisdom is wide-ranging. Here he thinks of it in relation to everyday living.

Wise behaviour
Wisdom is needed for a right walk. The Christian needs more than his own understanding. He especially needs it in deciding the use of his time.

Consider time as a precious commodity. How easy it is to waste it. The wise Christian constantly seeks God's guidance in the use of time. His yardstick is the Lord's will.

Spiritual enjoyment
Drunkenness was evidently a problem in the environment. Christians had to develop a different approach.

Drunkenness and debauchery are inseparably linked.

Enjoyment through wine is ephemeral and harmful. But a much greater and more wholesome enjoyment is available through the Spirit.

Social worship
Spiritual fullness expresses itself in various ways.
   (a) *Singing.* Psalms and hymns and spiritual songs were presumably different forms of worship. All strong spiritual movements express their joy through song. Christian faith was never intended to be drab.
   (b) *Thanksgiving.* 'Always' and 'for everything' are particularly comprehensive. Christians ought never to run dry of suitable subjects for praise. Note that all is to be done in the name of Christ.

In Christian thought and action, wisdom is essentially practical. The wise person is the person who lives wisely.

EPHESIANS 5:15, 16
Walking carefully

Paul has just urged his readers to expose the works of darkness. Those who reprove others must carefully watch their own step.

The necessity for a careful walk
The world around us is always watching our behaviour. The slightest slip is seized on. The Christian must be beyond reproach.

The nature of a careful walk
Everything is classified according to whether it is wise or foolish. The fool is careless because he does not recognise the importance of his moral life. Christian wisdom is seen in the quality of our moral decisions.

The demands of a careful walk

Paul sums it up as making the most of the time. This introduces a constant sense of urgency. The reason given is the evil of the days. This advice is still applicable.

> *Careless walk can only hamper the spread of the gospel. There is a constant need for Christians to recognise their responsibility.*

EPHESIANS 5:18
Drunkenness and its antidote

> *Drunkenness was a problem at Ephesus and elsewhere in Paul's world. Alcoholism is still a major problem in modern society. So often the spiritual answer to it is overlooked.*

Drunkenness

Paul sees it as one of the unfruitful works of darkness. There are many reasons why it should still be regarded in the same light.

It affects both mind and body. It leads to further degradation. It brings no more than the most fleeting pleasure.

A drunken person is a shame to humanity. Such lack of control cannot be countenanced by Christians.

Its antidote

In case any should think there is no adequate alternative, Paul speaks of being filled with the Spirit. This brings a more lasting sense of pleasure.

Such fullness never leads to lack of control, but rather to its opposite. It never produces further complications, but always develops gifts and fruits.

> *If alcoholism is a physical and moral problem of vast proportions, which pulls humanity down,*

spiritual fullness is a perfect antidote. No one can be full of the Spirit and full of wine at the same time.

EPHESIANS 5:19
Christian worship

This is a valuable passage for bringing out some important features of Christian worship.

It is spiritual
It is a manifestation of the fullness of the Spirit. The Spirit still leads people into worship.

It is emotional
Worship is said to be 'with all your heart'. This makes room for the emotions. Worship is not all theory – it must involve the whole person.

It is joyful
The psalms and hymns and spiritual songs have a joyful ring about them. Is our worship too often solemn?

It is melodious
When Paul speaks of making melody to the Lord, he means that worship aims to honour the Lord. What we do must be in keeping with that aim.

It is corporate
In one sense we assist one another in the way we worship. The great value of hymns and songs is that all can join together in the praise of God.

It is thankful
Worship should always begin with thanks. When we acknowledge that everything is from God, worship has already begun.

This is an ever relevant theme. We need constantly to check our patterns by Paul's words.

EPHESIANS 5:20
Thanksgiving

Thanksgiving is one of Paul's most familiar themes. It should also be a constant theme for all Christians.

Its timing
'Always'. This covers all life's programmes. Paul's own experiences were as varied as anyone's, and yet he sees the possibility of constant thanksgiving. There is no question of simply being thankful when we feel like it.

Its subjects
'Everything'. This is challenging and demanding. It includes all kinds of situations – some happy, some difficult, some even despairing.

Its method
It is directed to God. It is in the name of Christ. The thankful person always looks away from himself.

It may be that an examination of our thanksgiving sessions should follow from a meditation on Paul's statement.

EPHESIANS 5:21–33
Christian marriage

The relation between husbands and wives is used by Paul to teach some profound spiritual truths. This is an example where doctrine is found in the middle of practical advice.

A general principle
Paul's advice is 'be subject to one another'. This is applicable within the Christian community and even more so in

the case of a Christian husband and wife. Its basis is reverence for Christ.

The duties of wives

Paul does not hesitate to speak of obligations. The duty of subjection – a particular application of the general principle – is stressed.

The pattern here is spiritual. It is as to the Lord. The husband is seen through the relation between Christ and the church. We must bear in mind the great difference between the headship of the husband and the headship of the church – although there is an analogy.

The duties of husbands

Paul gives more detailed exhortation here.

- (a) They must love their wives. Marriage without love finds no place in Christian thought.
- (b) They must love as Christ loved the church. This involved sacrifice and sanctification. Its aim is to provide a blameless community.
- (c) They must love as they love their own bodies. This is also challenging for it eliminates pure self-love which is ruinous to any marriage. Again Paul calls on the analogy of Christ's love for the church. But he admits it to be a mystery.

If husbands really loved their wives in this manner,
it would remove all barriers to submission. The
husband would earn his wife's respect.

EPHESIANS 5:25–32
Christ and his church

*Paul introduces some statements about the church
in this passage, although his real theme is the
marriage relationship. The almost incidental
remarks are nevertheless of great value for the light
they throw on Paul's idea of the church.*

Christ is the head of the church

The headship of Christ establishes his Lordship over the
church. As the body can do nothing apart from the head, so
the church is dependent on Christ. But he is also the
Saviour. Christians owe everything to the head.

Christ prepares the church as a bride

(a) He loved the church.
(b) He gave himself for the church.
(c) He makes her holy and cleanses her.
(d) He intends to remove all spots and wrinkles.

Christ and the church are united together

As husband and wife are joined together to become one, so
Paul sees an analogy to the relation between Christ and the
church. He admits this is a great mystery. It certainly
stresses close relationship. This imagery is much more
personal than the cornerstone idea of 2:20.

*The more we weigh Paul's words, the more will the
preciousness of the church to Christ become
apparent.*

EPHESIANS 6:1–4
Children and parents

*Family relationships are particularly important for
Christians. The idea of duties has frequently
dropped from modern approaches.*

Duties of children

Paul mentions a twofold obligation towards parents.

(a) *Obedience.* An attitude of obedience is needed for
right training. But there is a condition – it is in the
Lord. Christian discipline is for the good of the child.

(b) *Honour.* The Old Testament law demands that children should honour parents. The commandment is
linked to a promise. Does this mean that all obedient
children will live long? Clearly not; but it suggests
that a well-ordered family life provides a good environment for the wellbeing of each member.

Duties of parents

There is a positive and a negative side.

(a) *Negative side.* Fathers are not to provoke to anger.
Hasty reactions can be harmful and do not achieve
positive results. A parent who displays anger is most
likely to provoke it in the children.

(b) *Positive side.* They are to bring children up in the
discipline and instruction of the Lord. The alarming
rise in juvenile crime would have been lessened if
more parents exercised discipline. Modern rejection
of home discipline cannot be supported by the
thoughtful Christian.

*Here is a subject which needs constant airing.
Paul's advice has not become outdated.*

EPHESIANS 6:5–9
Servants and masters

*In Paul's day slavery was widespread. This is the
nearest he gets to commenting on industrial
relations. His words still convey some important
principles. He is, of course, presenting a Christian
view of contemporary relationships.*

Servants and their duties

(a) The need for *obedience*. This was taken for granted
in an age of slavery. But wherever there is an em-
ployer-worker relationship, some authority must be
involved.

(b) The special *qualities* of Christian servants. Paul mentions fear and trembling, and singleness of heart.
The whole must be related to Christ.

Some may reject this as servile subservience. But
the Christian's duty is to follow Christ, who never
favoured anarchy.

(c) Special *attitudes* to avoid. Paul advises against 'eye-
service as men pleasers'. The Christian work ethic
demands more than keeping favour with men. It
means honouring Christ through work. The Christian sees everyday work as part of God's will.

Work is seen in the light of God's purpose. Today
some kinds of work would have to be excluded on
this principle (e.g. any which involved dishonest
practice).

(d) Special *recompense* promised. In a time of slavery, it
was difficult to recognise the category of spiritual
rewards. God will always honour the right attitude.
But this is no promise of material advantages for
those committed to God's will.

Masters and their duties

Paul sees clearly that those in control have their own
particular responsibilities.

(a) Christian masters must *pursue the good*. Paul is clear that there must not be two standards.
(b) Christians must *reject a threatening attitude*. They must not take unfair advantage of their position.
(c) They must reject *partiality*. Being impartial is a difficult exercise. But the Christian has a pattern. He has a master (God) who never shows partiality.

If more of these principles were introduced into modern industrial relations by Christian managers and employees, an example would be set which would have repercussions beyond the Christian community.

EPHESIANS 6:10–20
Christian warfare

Paul is deeply conscious of the spiritual battle. His whole missionary career illustrates this. But he also knows that all Christians are equally involved. He brings out some guiding principles for Christian strategy.

Know your resources
The strength needed is 'in the Lord'. This at once dispenses with human resources. If we enter the conflict trusting our own strength, disaster will follow.

Know your enemies
Intelligence is a vital part in all military operations. An army must know about the enemy's policies and strength. Paul has no doubt about our spiritual enemies:
(a) They are not flesh and blood.
(b) They are spiritual powers.
(c) They can be summed up as the wiles of the devil and of the hosts of wickedness in high places.
Those who ignore the devil are like a country which refuses to acknowledge that an enemy has declared war on it.

Know your equipment

In time of war, the Ministry of Defence constantly surveys its equipment. Indeed, it needs to update it. But in spiritual warfare it is always available and adequate.

Paul writes of armour, girdles, breastplates, footwear, shields, helmets and swords. The illustration is now outdated, but not the truths illustrated. Truth, righteousness, peace, faith, salvation and the word of God are timeless and effective.

Know your drill

Paul urges prayer and perseverance. Again there is reliance on God – in the Spirit. The spiritual warfare involves all the saints and Paul in particular. His need is for boldness in presenting the gospel.

Prayer may seem so passive as to be irrelevant to the conflict scene. But the battle is won behind the scenes.

Paul has no doubt about the outcome. He knows the devil is a defeated foe. Are we sufficiently convinced that we are on the winning side?

EPHESIANS 6:10
The strength of the Lord

On several occasions Paul comments on the resources which are available to Christians. Here he introduces us to spiritual strength.

Christians are never intended to be weak

This is the negative side. Paul does not argue that – he assumes it. The Christian challenge is tough and needs strong characters.

They must take steps to be strong

This is the positive side. It is in the form of an exhortation. Nevertheless we cannot make ourselves strong. This is one of Paul's paradoxes. We cannot be strong in ourselves – only in the Lord.

Their strength is not their own but the Lord's

The words 'in the strength of his might' resolves the paradox. In effect God says 'be strong', and then provides the strength.

The Christian church has suffered much through its members' weakness. But both individually and corporately Christians have the capacity to overcome all opposition.

EPHESIANS 6:11–17
The armour of God

When discussing the Christian's equipment, Paul introduces five defensive items and one attacking item. With so strong an enemy as the forces of evil, defence is crucial.
Note the positive injunctions – put on, take, stand, shod – all requiring a positive response. God's armour is for those who mean business.

The girdle of truth

The girded loins mean readiness for action. Truth will guard against unwary compromise. The Christian's standard is absolute – Christ is the truth.

The breastplate of righteousness

This item of armour protects the heart. Paul often speaks of the righteousness of God (Rom. 1:17; 3:21, 25). This is not open to negotiation. The devil cannot touch those resting in God's righteousness.

The sandals of peace

Military sandals supplied a good grip for steady walking. Paul thinks of the peace which comes through the gospel in a similar way. The Christian warrior needs constant peace of mind.

The shield of faith

The shield was manoeuvrable to combat arrows. Paul thinks of the constant barrage of evil in such terms. Faith in God is faith in one who is greater than the devil. True faith denies any advantage to the adversary.

The helmet of salvation

This is another protective armament. Salvation is a broad term to describe the benefits of the gospel. Those saved through Christ are lost to the devil.

The sword of the Spirit

The sword is the only offensive weapon mentioned here. It is the work of the Spirit and consists of the word of God. Knowledge of the word is essential to put to flight the forces of darkness (cf. Rev. 19:15; Heb. 4:12).

The armour is exactly designed for protection and attack in conflict against spiritual enemies. It never becomes obsolete and never suffers defeat.

EPHESIANS 6:18–20
Prayer

Paul's usual way of teaching about prayer is by giving samples of his own. But here he gives more direct advice.

Its frequency
At all times.

Its basis
In the Spirit

Its nature
Prayer and supplication.

Its persistence
With all perseverance.

Its scope
For all the saints and for Paul in his preaching.

This powerful prayer is concentrating on the progress and proclamation of the gospel.

EPHESIANS 6:19, 20
An ambassador's request

An ambassador is in a privileged position. Paul uses this idea, but applies it in a surprising way.

His position
The chains do not cancel out the office. In a sense the chains showed the determination which Paul had put into his task. His effectiveness had been noticed.

His aims
His task was to preach the mystery of the gospel openly. He saw that mystery as now wide open. His burden was for others to hear it.

His request
Not material resources – but prayer. Is that the best his readers can do? Indeed is there anything else? Through their prayer he could effectively open his mouth.

What was true of Paul is true for all witnesses of the gospel. Do we sufficiently recognise the privilege of sharing with others in their work?

EPHESIANS 6:21–24
Paul's conclusion

*As the beginnings of Paul's letters are varied and
fascinating, so are his endings.*

His respected representative
Tychicus is described as (a) beloved brother, (b) faithful
minister. He was clearly a person highly esteemed by Paul
who regards him as thoroughly dependable.

His special task was to inform about Paul's affairs. Paul
places great emphasis on others knowing his movements
and his needs.

Communications are necessary for encouragement.
Christians were intended to have mutual concern.

His benediction
This is particularly strong because it is threefold.
(a) *Peace to the brethren.* This is a comprehensive concluding prayer. The hallmark of the gospel is peace
and this is to be shared among the brethren.
(b) *Love with faith.* Faith without love is cold and un-
inviting. But this love springs from faith in Christ. It
is a reflection of God's love in Christ. It comes from
both God the Father and the Lord Jesus Christ.
(c) *Grace to all.* This is the natural consequence of the
last point. Those who love Christ are those who have
experienced his grace.

*Grace and peace are mentioned at the beginning of
this letter. These Christian qualities are still in
mind at the end.*

PHILIPPIANS
Introduction

About Philippi

Philippi was a city founded by Philip of Macedon, the father of Alexander the Great. The Roman Octavian, who became the Emperor Augustus, established a military colony there in 31 B.C. Those who belonged to this city received citizen status, which carried with it special privileges.

About the church

On Paul's first visit there a Jewish proselyte named Lydia and the gaoler and his household were converted. A demon-possessed girl was exorcised (Acts 16). Others definitely connected with the church were Epaphroditus, Euodia, Syntyche and Clement (Phil. 2:25 ff.; 4:2, 3). The church's officers were bishops and deacons (Phil. 1:1).

About the purpose of the letter

Paul mentions the gifts which the Philippians had sent to him (4:18). He refers to the partnership which he had with them in the gospel (1:5), possibly an allusion to the same thing. Paul naturally wants to tell them how much he appreciates the help they have given to him.

Moreover, Epaphroditus, a Philippian who had been of great assistance to Paul, had been ill and was returning home. This provided the apostle with an excellent opportunity to write to the church. He wanted them to know that both he and Timothy hoped to visit them soon.

About the writer

Paul refers to his imprisonment in 1:7, 13, 16. This assists us in visualising the circumstances in which the letter was written. In spite of being a prisoner, Paul's constant theme in this letter is one of joy, which shows how his indomitable spirit could triumph over the most adverse circumstances. Far from crushing him, the experience enabled him to write what is probably his most affectionate letter.

About the date
From Phil. 1:19–26 it appears that Paul faces the possibility of death. This factor would fit in well with a date at the end of the Roman imprisonment mentioned in Acts 28:30, so about A.D. 59. Some have inclined to the view that Paul may have been imprisoned at Ephesus and that the latter could have been written from there, i.e. five or six years earlier.

PHILIPPIANS 1:1, 2
Address and salutation

There is a certain individuality about the way that Paul begins each of his letters. They are worth careful consideration.

Paul's description of himself
(a) It is noticeable that he does not describe himself as an apostle, as was his usual custom. He does not wish to overemphasise his authority in this case.
(b) He prefers to call Timothy and himself 'servants of Christ Jesus'.

His description of the Philippians
(a) He calls them 'saints', i.e. holy ones. This is the potential of believers.
(b) Saints are such because they are 'in Christ'. Note that the bishops and deacons are mentioned after the saints. The order of mention is not insignificant. Paul is writing to the whole community.

The greeting
This is a sample of what Christian greetings should be.
(a) *Grace.* This is clearly a greeting which is related to God's free favour to man.
(b) *Peace.* This is again a quality derived specifically from God.

These two greetings were normal in the ancient world, but Paul takes them and invests them with spiritual meaning.

PHILIPPIANS 1:3–11
Paul's prayer for other Christians

So much prayer is self-centred that it is good to focus on others. Paul shows the way. His prayer finds strong reason to thank God. The following points can be a valuable pattern for prayer.

His thankfulness for their fellowship
Their partnership in the gospel probably went further than financial aid. All along they were in sympathy with Paul's aims in spreading the gospel (4:14ff.).

He thanks God for such partnership. Note especially the constancy and persistence of Paul's thanksgiving.

His assurance about God's purpose for them
Paul knows that God has begun the good work. The principle here is that God cannot leave his work incomplete. Paul cannot conceive that God's plans can fail.

His appreciation of their help
They were partakers with him of grace. Both he and they shared the same gospel. The Philippians had a real share in his bonds. The true expression of appreciation is seen in the words 'I hold you in my heart'.

His desire for their development
He calls on God as witness – so convinced was he of the rightness of his yearning for them. That yearning here is linked with Christ's love.

His prayer is for increasing love, knowledge and discernment. He also wants them to be blameless in the day of Christ and to be fruitful now. This is an excellent example of a large-hearted prayer.

Paul's prayer for others is a powerful pattern for all Christians, especially for Christian workers. In Paul's approach to prayer others always took precedence over self. Our aim should be to develop a similar mentality.

PHILIPPIANS 1:3–11
Gratitude, hope and prayer

*Here the apostle brings together three important
features of the Christian life.*

Gratitude

(a) *The person addressed.* Paul recognises that God is
the source of everything and he therefore addresses
his thanks to him. Note the personal aspect here – he
uses the words 'my God'.

(b) *The basis.* Paul had experienced the co-operation of
the Philippians. It was not hearsay, but first-hand
knowledge.

(c) *The method.* When Paul uses such words as 'all my
remembrance', 'in every prayer' and 'for you all', it is
clear that his thankfulness is remarkably comprehensive.

(d) *The content.* He especially appreciates their partnership with him. They were together sharers in the
gospel.

Hope

The apostle's 'I am sure' springs from a deep conviction
that God is at work. His confidence was well based.

(a) *The work was good.* God's work is always good
because he himself is good.

(b) *The work had already begun.* Whenever people become Christians, it is God's work. Paul is convinced
that all spiritual change follows from God's initiative.

(c) *The work was continuing.* The process of transformation is an on-going one. Christians are not yet
perfect.

(d) *The work will be completed.* God cannot leave his
work half done. A completion date is certain. Paul
sees this date as the day of the second coming, i.e.
'the day'.

Prayer
The burden of the prayer is for a multiplication of love. He knows all Christians need this. No one has too much of it.

(a) *It will affect knowledge and discernment.* Paul is not thinking of the emotion of love divorced from the mind. The highest type of love leads to the ennobling of thought.

(b) *It will promote a quest for excellence.* Christian love sets its sights high. It desires nothing less than the best. Approving what is excellent means seeking it as the standard of attainment.

(c) *It will bring about positive results.* Paul talks about purity and about the fruits of righteousness. If Paul's prayer is answered it will be for God's glory.

To follow so rich an example will enrich our own characters and at the same time will enrich others.

PHILIPPIANS 1:3–8
An example for Christian workers

The Christian church has always regarded Paul and his teaching as an inspiration. Here in the opening to this letter we have an example of his approach to those he has won for Christ.

His memory of his converts
He kept them vividly in his mind.

His prayer for them
This was comprehensive and constant.

His humility before God
He never supposed his converts were a credit to himself.

His sincere love for his converts
There is evidence of a deep love, comparable to Christ's
love for him.

*We may feel we can never emulate the apostle, but
we can learn from his example.*

PHILIPPIANS 1:3–5
Thanksgiving

*Most of Paul's letters begin with thanksgiving.
This shows the great importance he attached to it.*

A natural exercise for the believer
Paul points the way as an example for all.

An exercise depending on memory
We cannot be thankful unless we can recall what God is
doing.

An exercise without limits
Paul provides a fine example of unrestrictedness in his
prayer.

An exercise prompted by fellowship
There was a partnership which filled Paul with joy.

*Thankful Christians are undoubtedly a delight to
God. We should compare our level of
thanksgiving with that of Paul.*

PHILIPPIANS 1:6–8
Paul and the Philippians

It is valuable to reflect on Paul's relations to his readers. In each letter we gain different insights.

His strong confidence in God's plan for them
   (a) The plan was good.
   (b) The plan was radical – it was within them.
   (c) The plan was supernatural.
   (d) The plan was continual – until the final day.

His strong sympathy with them
   (a) They occupied his thoughts.
   (b) They filled his heart.
   (c) They caused him to yearn for them – with all the affection of Christ.

This is a kind of personal testimony by the apostle of his approach to other people and serves as a pattern for us.

PHILIPPIANS 1:9–11
The value of Christian love

The apostle has a great deal to say about love in his epistles.

It is the main theme of Paul's prayer
Paul always accepted the primacy of love.

It always provides scope for more love
Paul is not satisfied with the minimum. He asks for abundance.

It is inseparably linked with knowledge
Love needs linking with right understanding. Paul has no place for mindless love.

It leads to added discernment
Discernment is the right use of knowledge.

It promotes purity
Man's quest must always be for a purity like that of Christ.

It produces fruit
Love is most productive. It never has a failed harvest.

There is no denying the value of love. What is more difficult is the fostering of it. Every meditation centred on it should deepen our desire to put it into practice.

PHILIPPIANS 1:9–11
Christian improvement

No one can read Paul's letters without being impressed with his intense desire for the maturing of his readers in the Christian life.

In the realm of knowledge
Knowledge must be seen to lead to discernment. This is the wise use of knowledge.

In the approval of what is excellent
There are two stages here – recognition of excellence and the approving of it.

In the quest for sincerity
Purity of mind and motive is a constant Christian goal.

In being without offence
Blamelessness can be achieved only through Christ.

In the application of righteousness
The fruits are reproduced through living in Christ.

Whatever improvements are attained by Christians, the result is greater praise and glory to God.

PHILIPPIANS 1:12–30
Paul reflects on his captivity

Adverse circumstances often lead to unexpected results. Paul's experiences may prompt us to think of examples from our own lives.

He rejoices in the progress of the gospel in Rome
He reflects on the effects of his adversity.
   (a) It has led to the advancement of the gospel.
   (b) It has provided increased publicity.
   (c) It has increased the courage of his companions.
   (d) It has given rise to conflicting motives.
   (e) It has produced a Christ-centred approach.
Paul rejoices that Christ has been preached. He rejoices in his own salvation. He is convinced that he has no reason to be ashamed.

He considers the question of life and death
Paul's circumstances have forced him to consider this important theme.
   (a) He notes the gain involved in dying. He reflects that he had already had a relationship with Christ. For him death will only advance that relationship.
   (b) He recognises that others will gain if he continues to live.
   (c) His preference is for the advantage of others. He desires their progress in the faith. He longs for their joy in the faith. He wants them to glory in Christ Jesus.

He encourages worthy Christian living

(a) The standard for Christian living is the gospel.

(b) It is independent of Paul's presence.

(c) It is seen in two specific Christian duties.
The first is unity. They were to stand fast in one mind.
The second is fearlessness. They were not to be frightened by their opponents.

(d) Paul sees the Philippians as sharing his sufferings. This suggests that no Christian can claim exemption from an element of suffering.

These comments of Paul's arise from his own experience. Everything is for Christ's sake.

PHILIPPIANS 1:12–18
Paul and the advance of the gospel

Paul's dominating concern was for the gospel. He was devoted to its advance. This meant its proclamation and application. After his prayer and thanksgiving he introduces his first theme. Note his strong desire for his readers (his brethren) to be informed.

Adverse circumstances did not deter him

He reflects on what had happened to him (cf. 2 Cor. 11). Few have encountered so much for the sake of the gospel.

Our approach to circumstances reveals much about our character. Paul balances the evidence and concludes for advance. He was not swayed by personal convenience.

(a) *His chains attracted attention.* The whole palace guard heard about it. It had news value. The effect of it was an encouragement to Paul as he felt his chains.

(b) *His chains encouraged others.* It seems a disaster –

the great missionary apostle chained up! But many had become confident in the Lord. See how positive Paul is!

His example prompted others to witness

Most important to Paul was the preaching of the gospel.

(a) *Much preaching activity*. What he could not do others were doing.

(b) *Yet different motives*. Pure motives. Good will and love. What an encouragement to know that others were continuing the good work.

Impure motives. Envy, rivalry, partisanship, pretence. Was Paul exaggerating? Were there those who wanted to distress him? It may seem hard to believe, but this kind of thing is not uncommon.

He rejoices whenever Christ is preached

Most would write the rivals off, or at least dissociate from them. But Paul has a large heart. How many would rejoice in a similar situation? It would be so natural to denounce.

Here the apostle demonstrates his great spiritual maturity. The preaching of Christ took precedence over Paul's personal feelings.

For Paul Christ was the touchstone. His own circumstances and reactions were secondary. Let us seek to emulate his example.

PHILIPPIANS 1:15–18
Differences among preachers and how to deal with them

Paul's situation presents some principles of action which can be applied in a variety of other circumstances. We shall look at this passage to discover ways and means of dealing with differences among those who preach the gospel.

The different spirit of two classes of preacher

It is not enough to note that various people are preaching Christ. We need to acknowledge differences of motive. Too often we tend towards stereotypes. But it is valuable to analyse where the differences lie.

The motives which explain the differences

It must be admitted that personality problems often affect the preachers of the gospel.

(a) *The pure motives of one class*. There were those who had a genuine love for Paul. Their aim was to make up for his lack of opportunity to preach.

(b) *The impure motives of the other class*. These showed a lack of concern for Paul.

(c) *Yet both groups preached Christ*. Paul does not question the preaching content of the second group. He is convinced that others are learning about Christ.

The joy which should result from this activity

Paul shows the way. A lesser man would have resented and challenged the motives of the second group. They thought they would harm Paul, but he rises above their pettiness. To be able to rejoice in the circumstances shows the true measure of the man.

If Paul's large-heartedness had been the dominant pattern in Church history, much greater progress would have been made. Are we able to rejoice in the preaching of the gospel, whoever does it?

PHILIPPIANS 1:18
Preaching prompted by jealousy

Some attach great importance to motive in the preaching of the gospel. Undoubtedly motive is important, but is it the most important?

Preaching Christ is the church's most important work
This was the apostle's conviction. The whole New Testament testifies to the same thing.

Christ can be preached in a variety of ways
  (a) It is important to be sure that Christ is truly being preached.
  (b) Agreement over this must take precedence over differences of method.
  (c) The truth of the gospel is more important than personalities or motives.

Even divisions can lead to more zealous preaching
It would be better for this to happen than to have stagnant agreement with no zest.

The whole passage demonstrates that the gospel is greater than its preachers.

PHILIPPIANS 1:19–26
The dilemma

Dilemmas are a part of life. Some are overwhelmed when choices have to be made. But Paul even creates a theoretical dilemma.

A discussion about honouring Christ
Paul's supreme aim was to honour Christ. This affected his whole approach to life, including his body.
  (a) *Paul continues his rejoicing.* The note of rejoicing is

sounded throughout the epistle even when Paul is dealing with the subject of death. This should provide a pattern for us.

(b) *He is convinced of the value of other people's prayers*. Note how Paul links prayer and the Spirit's help or supply.

(c) *He is expecting deliverance*. Paul's confidence is in God, not in himself. He knows that all will turn out right if God is in control.

(d) *He wants to be unashamed*. His eager expectation and hope are expressed in strong terms. His desire to be unashamed applies both to life and to death. This leads him into his dilemma theme.

The great dilemma

It was not a real choice. But the exercise helped to clarify the issues.

(a) *A statement of the alternatives*.

To live. Paul sums it up in one word, Christ. For him everything had to be governed by Christ. How do we measure up to this?

To die. This Paul summarises as gain. How can death be gain? Verse 28 gives the answer.

Either way Paul could not lose.

(b) *An enlargement of the first alternative*. Life would mean fruitful labour. Paul's thought is dominated by others. As long as life lasts Paul thinks in terms of work.

(c) *An enlargement of the second alternative*. Death means being with Christ – which Paul sees as far better. To be in the presence of Christ is a glorious prospect.

(d) *The dilemma*. The apostle is hard pressed to choose. He concludes for life. But God did not leave the choice to him.

(e) *The resultant attitude to life*. Paul puts death out of his mind and thinks of life. The believers' progress and joy are involved. They have good cause for rejoicing.

Out of the imaginary dilemma Paul's insights were deepened. This could provide a useful exercise for us.

PHILIPPIANS 1:21
The alternatives

Most people have problems about life and death.
Paul sets out the Christian answer.

Christian living has its supreme object in Christ
(a) Christ dominated all Paul's thoughts. To be 'in Christ' is to have full Christian experience.
(b) He also controlled all Paul's work. Christ was central in Paul's proclamation.

Christian dying is seen as gain
(a) It is difficult to reconcile this with human feelings, but Paul is convinced of its truth.
(b) Such a conviction banishes pessimism, for both life and death offer expectations of positive achievement.
(c) Such a conviction shows the true connection between life and death.

Living becomes so much more exciting when death
can be welcomed.

PHILIPPIANS 1:22–26
Self love and social love

This is an exercise in self versus others. It is
relevant in so many situations that it repays careful
consideration.

Self love desired escape
Paul's view of death is as a release from present trials and as an entrance into Christ's presence. He is convinced that death is far better than earthly existence. It is his strong personal conviction.

Social love urged continuance

Paul is a realist. Service to others is possible only while life lasts. His departure would remove a valuable servant of God from his church.

Social love was more powerful than self love

Paul inclined towards remaining for the sake of others – in spite of more labours and undoubtedly more hardships.

We may use Paul's deliberations as a spur to discover where our priorities lie.

PHILIPPIANS 1:27–30
A life worthy of the gospel

Paul is concerned about the manner in which the Philippians conduct their lives irrespective of what happened to him. He provides some indications of what constitutes a worthy life.

A firm witness

Standing firm and contending for the gospel show a clear and definite commitment. There is no place here for indecision. Believers are expected to show solidarity in contending for the faith.

Unity

There are many expressions here for the idea of oneness. 'In one spirit' and 'as one man' show the importance Paul attached to Christian unity. He develops it further in Chapter 2.

Fearlessness

Those with a positive approach to witness will have to come to terms with opponents of the gospel. Paul advises fearlessness because deliverance is finally in God's hands.

Readiness to suffer

The Philippians had already known persecution. It was similar to Paul's own experience. What is done 'on Christ's behalf' may or may not involve suffering. But Christians must be prepared.

The gospel of Christ makes demands on its adherents. Doctrine must have some effect upon life.

PHILIPPIANS 1:29, 30
The privilege of suffering

Throughout Christian history Christians have been persecuted. Paul offers some encouragement here. It is never easy to regard hardship as a privilege.

Suffering for Christ is regarded as a gift

Paul here uses a word meaning to grant a favour.

(a) God gives the ability to endure suffering.
(b) He is honoured through his people's suffering.
(c) He rewards his people for their endurance.

Faith in Christ must precede suffering for him

Christians must first be identifiable as believers in Christ. Only such people can suffer *for* him.

Encouragement through the example of Christ

Shared sufferings are always easier to bear. The Philippians and Paul were in the same situation. There is strength in the fellowship of suffering.

This passage should encourage us to face suffering for Christ, if called upon to do so, in the same spirit.

PHILIPPIANS 2:1–4
The importance of unity

So many modern influences promote division because they set one group against another. In view of this it is good to contemplate the Christian concept of unity. Paul has already mentioned this in Philippians 1.

Paul's desire for his readers

Unity is clearly a theme of importance for Paul.

(a) *Their state affected his.* In pursuing unity they will fulfil his joy. It is important to note that what affects the body of Christ affects every member.

(b) *His desire is based on Christ's desire.* Paul's love for them is prompted by Christ's love for them. The affection of Christ is a powerful motive.

(c) *His desire finds expression in unity.* The whole passage throbs with this theme.

All in positions of Christian leadership should note the importance Paul attaches to this theme.

Motives which should promote unity

(a) *Life in Christ.* Every Christian has the indwelling Christ. This should lead to oneness in him.

(b) *Christian love.* Paul rates this as the highest gift (cf. 1 Cor. 13). Love binds and does not divide.

(c) *The Holy Spirit.* Paul speaks of fellowship through the Spirit. Fellowship demands some basis of unity and this is achieved only through the Spirit.

(d) *Christian compassion.* Clearly allied to love but bringing out more emphasis on tender concern for others.

Humility as an essential ingredient of unity

With such powerful motives, what hinders unity? Paul's answer is pride. Hence the need for humility.

(a) *Factions destroy unity.* Party spirit is a great spoiler. Strife, according to Gal. 5:20, is a work of the flesh.

(b) *Vain-glory puts self before unity*. This refers to the wrong kind of ambition.

(c) *Humility puts others before self*. Paul expresses the ideal in terms of esteeming others more highly, an attitude which calls for considerable humility.

(d) *Humility considers the needs of others as well as its own*. This is the practical side of verse 3. Esteem for others is inseparable from concern about their affairs.

Several important lessons emerge. We should strive for unity. We should rejoice in the progress of others. We should not be afraid positively to develop humility.

PHILIPPIANS 2:1–4
Genuine socialism

Man is not an isolated individual. He must relate to others. What contribution can Christian teaching make?

Christian community centres on a common object of love

The uniting factor is Christ. Human efforts at community are not divorced from self. This is the spiritual aspect which human systems ignore.

Christian ideals demand a strong element of humility

This quality is not much sought after. The Greeks and most modern cultures have depised it. It is the antithesis of 'every man for himself'.

Christian social concern is a duty

Many Christians fail to take verse 4 seriously. It does not require the rejection of all self-interest, but it does set a high standard for social concern. A philosophy which includes others as well as self is demanding, especially in a time of social need.

The application of true Christian principles must lead to a genuine concern for others.

PHILIPPIANS 2:1, 2
The Christian view of like-mindedness

Is like-mindedness possible? Paul uses several expressions to describe it. He clearly recognised its desirability.

Its nature

(a) *It is centred in love*. Those who have the same love grow into a common likeness. There develops a powerful bond which promotes unity.

(b) *It affects the intellect*. Unity of mind is more difficult to attain. In what sense is intellectual uniformity involved? Some intellectual and doctrinal harmony is necessary for true unity. But this must allow for differences over non-basic positions. Consider the significance of this in approaches to doctrinal bases of faith.

(c) *It involves common aims*. True like-mindedness can be achieved only when harmony of purpose is evident (cf. 2 Cor. 6:14ff).

Its grounds

Verse 2 depends on verse 1, which brings out several common features.

(a) *Common experience 'in Christ'*. Paul is speaking of Christian like-mindedness which presupposes a common basis. All Christians must equally consider the same exhortation.

(b) *Common source of comfort.* Those who need sympathetic support find it most easily among those they love.

(c) *Common sharing of the Spirit.* There is an instinctive oneness among those controlled by the Spirit of God.

(d) *Common tenderness.* Unity of mind is more likely to follow from compassion than from criticism.

Real Christian like-mindedness, which is to be distinguished from uniformity, is a constant source of joy.

PHILIPPIANS 2:3, 4
Unity and how to achieve it

The quest for unity is an age-old quest. Some have achieved it by the use of force – but such unity is only superficial. Paul knows a better way and expresses it both negatively and positively.

The negative side
Concentrate on the causes of disunity. A right diagnosis of the disease will assist a cure.

(a) *Strife.* The opposite of unity and therefore a striking reminder of the urgent need for unity.

(b) *Vain-glory.* Personal vanity is generally disruptive. It is committed to promoting self.

The positive side
Paul gives two considerations which help us in the quest for unity.

(a) *Humility.* The opposite of vain-glory. This is much more difficult to achieve.

118

(b) *Consideration for others*. This is the opposite of strife. Placing others above self is a radical challenge.

The natural man has a negative bias. Only the Christian faith can produce a positive bias, because it produces a change of heart.

PHILIPPIANS 2:4
Selfishness

Selfishness means living for ourselves and always putting self before anyone else. It is uniformly condemned in the Christian way of life.

It affects the whole person
It influences thought, feeling and action. It leads to a variety of sins.

Christian faith regards it as unacceptable
Paul does not argue for this – he assumes it. Christ is the supreme example of selflessness.

For Christians 'others' must take precedence
We must be ready to look away from our own affairs. Our centre of interest should be elsewhere.

Christ demands a complete reappraisal of the importance of self.

PHILIPPIANS 2:5–11
The supreme example

Paul has been urging humility as the key to unity.
Many would regard this as unrealistic. How could
he expect people to develop such a quality?
This leads him into a profound reflection about
Christ. Note how doctrinal statements arise out of
practical needs, not in this case vice versa.

Christian imitation

Whether the words read 'Have the same mind which was
also in Christ Jesus' or, 'which you have in Christ Jesus', his
example is clearly in mind.

To be effective, imitation needs an adequate pattern.
Paul can think of none better than Christ himself. Humiliation is at the heart of the Christian message.

The perfect pattern

Christ is the unique fulfilment of the demand in verse 4. We
may first think of his disregard for himself and then of his
great regard for others.

   (a) *His rightful status.* There is here a high view of
       Christ.

       1. In the form of God. There is much discussion over
          the meaning, but some idea of equality with God
          is undeniable. He perfectly showed what God
          is.

       2. Yet he did not snatch at equality. If he was really
          equal with God he had no need to snatch at it. He
          did not in fact assert his right. That would have
          been vain-glory.

   (b) *His self-limitation.* It is important to note the volun-
       tary nature of this.

       1. The emptying. Whatever this means it shows that
          becoming man involved restrictions for Christ. It
          is the very opposite of self-seeking.

       2. The form of a servant. There was a dramatic

change of form – an acceptance of a servant role. This was the lowest form of living, comparable to that of slaves. It highlights Christ's amazing condescension.

3. The likeness of men. The true humanity of Jesus is implied in his servant role. It is stressed here to provide a perfect example for us.

4. The self-humbling. This shows the special relevance of Christ's example. This is humility par excellence.

5. The obedience of death. The cross is introduced, not to explain our salvation, but to demonstrate Christ's perfect obedience to God. No Christian will ever have greater humiliation than his master.

The resultant reward

The question must be faced whether humiliation is self-defeating. Is an act which ended in death credible? Clearly the result is of vital interest.

(a) *The exaltation was a divine act.* The New Testament makes clear that God raised him. In a sense, the sequence to death was out of his hands. The exaltation was of the highest quality. There is a parallel here with the enthronement theme. There could be no higher exaltation than God's throne.

(b) *The exaltation involved a new name.* The name matched the nature. No doubt the new name was LORD. Christians use the name in prayer. This was a demonstration of sovereignty. In what sense is this an example to us? Only in the sense that God acknowledges those who obey him.

(c) *The exaltation will lead to universal homage.* Verses 10 and 11 look to the future. All knees and all tongues will acknowledge the Lordship of Christ. The humble will live to see others humbled before him.

(d) *The exaltation ends in God's glory.* Many cannot see how the shame of the cross can ever lead to glory.

But Paul's deep conviction is supported elsewhere in the New Testament.

There is a paradox in Paul's train of thought. Christ achieved his end in a way totally opposed to the self-striving of the world. His method is the pattern for the Christian.

PHILIPPIANS 2:5–11
The development of a Christ-like spirit

This passage sets out what is involved in a Christ-like spirit. It must be the aim of every Christian to become more like Christ.

It involves self-denial

This is seen (a) in what Christ did not do, and (b) in what he did.

(a) *What Christ did not do*. The non-snatching approach of Christ is a challenge to all Christians. Yet for him it meant an infinitely greater self-denial than for us.

(b) *What Christ did*. The servant pattern involves doing things for others. The obedience pattern means complete conformity to God's will. The cross pattern points to the crucifying of self.

It means appreciation of a supreme name

It is an exalted name in which Christians can glory. It is a name that others will ultimately recognise. It is a name which glorifies God.

It is a privilege and an honour to bear the name of Christ and to share his Spirit. This is the way to become like him.

PHILIPPIANS 2:5–8
Self-sacrifice

Human history shows many examples of self-sacrifice. These are always inspiring. But nothing can match the self-giving of Christ. With him there is a unique sequence.

Equality
Self-giving must be judged by what is given. Jesus was not just a man. No other man had the 'form of God' as he had. His self-giving is correspondingly greater than any other.

Emptying
He could not lay aside his deity, but he restricted its operations. This was the supreme act of giving.

Becoming human
It is impossible to conceive of a greater transformation than the change from pre-existence to man. This is the measure of Christ's self-sacrifice.

Facing death
The death of an eternal person is inconceivable. But the death of man is normal. Christ received human life in order to give it up.

Facing an ignominious death
This was the worst and cruellest death that man could devise. Paul puts it – 'even the death of the cross'.

These five stages show the ultimate act of self-sacrifice against which all other sacrificial acts must be measured.

PHILIPPIANS 2:9–11
Exaltation

Christ's death was not the end. The sequel of that death is vital for Christian faith.

Christ's exaltation was prompted by his humiliation
He came from highest glory to lowest death. He returned to even greater glory, having accomplished his mission.

It was marked by a new name
He received a superlative name (Lord) which he alone could bear in its fullest sense.

It will be acknowledged by everyone
Bowed knees and confessing tongues will proclaim his greatness.

It shows him to be sovereign Lord
That 'Jesus Christ is Lord' will not only be a Christian confession, but a universal homage.

It brings great glory to the Father
It is the purpose of the Son to glorify the Father. Whenever men worship the Son, the Father is honoured.

Our Saviour is exalted above all others. Christians should rejoice in his wonderful name.

PHILIPPIANS 2:12, 13
The implications of following Christ's example

Before following anyone it is vital to know what is involved. We are not intended to be left in the dark. It is particularly important to know the implications of following Christ in view of his radical approach to self-sacrifice.

Obedience

It is not accidental that Christ's own obedience is mentioned in verse 8. That is the first lesson for all Christians.

The Philippians have already learned it. Yet it must be developed. It must also be acted upon whether Paul is present or not. This shows it to be of the essence of the Christian faith.

Disobedience and faith are not conducive. Lack of obedience at once weakens faith.

Effort

This may seem surprising. We may think that God's effort is enough. But Paul here stresses man's responsibility.

(a) *Working out salvation* cannot mean that Christ's work is unfinished. He came to bring salvation. His humiliation and exaltation was to this end. Our effort must be to apply what Christ has already done.

(b) *The effort is an individual matter,* which means that no one else can work it out for us. We must each work out our own salvation.

(c) *Yet salvation is a double work.* We can only work out what God has already worked in us. Consider what God has accomplished in the believer. We have every encouragement to apply ourselves. We could not do it except through God's resources.

Awe

Fear and trembling are not usually considered to be part of Christian living. Yet we lose much if we do not have a sense of awe. Two considerations will promote this:

(a) The greatness of the cost of our salvation should fill us with ceaseless wonder.
(b) The weakness of our own capabilities should equally fill us with awe.

Christian fear should of course be distinguished sharply from terror. What God is doing is for his own pleasure. That pleasure is the salvation of his people.

Paul's statement introduces a solemn note which is intended to spur us on, not to overwhelm us.

PHILIPPIANS 2:12, 13
Individual salvation

The New Testament view of salvation is concerned with the whole man. The word 'salvation' expresses the totality of what God has done to meet man's need. But it is important to see salvation in personal terms.

Salvation is the possession of every Christian

Paul does not establish this point. He assumes it.

The Philippians had already obeyed. They were Christians who had already been saved. They had had experience of God's grace.

Salvation is a continual work of God in the Christian

Conversion is only the beginning. God is still at work carrying out his purposes.

It should be noted that willing and doing are inseparable in God. His delight is to complete his saving work.

Salvation is accomplished only with man's co-operation

God could have done it without our help. But he does not treat us as robots. He works in us and expects us to work it out.

We cannot sit back and expect things to happen automatically. Much of the richness of the gospel must be diligently applied with a due sense of awe.

Our salvation is too great to trifle with. How sad if we fail to enjoy it to the full!

PHILIPPIANS 2:12, 13
Responsibility

Some passages bring special challenges. They make the reader take stock of his situation. This passage is of this type.

Remember the past

Reminiscence has its value. If experience has taught us anything, we should not forget it. Earlier experience of obedience should make it easier to continue to obey.

Face the present

At no time do we get beyond the need to work out our salvation. The seriousness of this is seen in the fear and trembling.

Our task should be to do God's will in order to bring pleasure to him.

God has not planned for a community of lazy-bones, but for seriously minded dedicated workers.

PHILIPPIANS 2:14–18
Lights at Philippi

The idea of Christians as lights in the world is familiar from Matt. 5:16. The New Testament frequently thinks of the world as moral darkness which needs spiritual illumination. Here Paul thinks of the positive contribution of some of his converts.

How to develop a right approach

Christians must exhibit a certain moral calibre. They must show a different approach from that of the world.

(a) *In the matter of relationships.* Many would consider that advice to live 'without murmurings or disputings' to be a weak approach. So many issues demand confrontation.

But Paul seems to be thinking here of murmurings against God. He is appealing for a peaceful and contented approach.

(b) *In the matter of reputations.* Christians are to be 'blameless and harmless', i.e. pure-minded, not affected by ulterior motives. This will make them stand out in an adverse environment. They must never be known as devious.

Others may blame Christians wrongly, but true blamelessness in the sight of God can have an effect on others.

(c) *In the matter of status.* Christians are adopted into a new family. They are sons of God. Sons should stand out in a world of slaves.

Whatever the world thinks, they should never lose sight of their true status.

How to be lights in a dark place

With the right approach just set out, Christians can shine as lights.

(a) *Because the environment is so dark.* It is described as crooked and perverse. This does not deny that any good can be found in it.

But the general ethos is crooked – it is not governed by the norm of righteousness. Its general standard is what is expedient.

(b) *Because the Christian can hold out the word of life.* The word which points to Christ is the source of all spiritual life.

The world may not receive what is being handed out, but it desperately needs it.

How to bring joy to God's servants

Paul reflects on the day of Christ. By this he means the day of Christ's coming, a day of reckoning.

(a) *He wants to rejoice then over his converts.* He even uses the word 'boast'. He expects his converts to be such notable lights that he will be able to boast over them.

(b) *He is willing to sacrifice much to this end.* He uses sacrificial language. He sees himself as a drink-offering. He is glad if his work is fruitful.

(c) *He thinks his converts should rejoice with him.* What greater joy is there when God's servants and their converts can rejoice together!

Wherever the light of the gospel shines, it always brings joy to the people of God.

PHILIPPIANS 2:14–16
Activity for God

An inactive church is never according to God's plan. The effectiveness of a Christian group must be gauged by its impact on its environment.

The attitude which should accompany the activity

Many churches begin with action and neglect attitude. Paul

has a sounder priority. If wrong attitudes persist, action will aggravate them.

   (a) *Uncomplaining*. Paul warns against discontentment. The murmuring spirit is damaging.

   (b) *Uncontentious*. Some seize on small points of difference to enlarge them into main issues. Paul sees clearly the danger of this.

   (c) *Irreproachable*. This means without fault and manifestly sincere.

Examine these moral demands before beginning any action.

The sphere in which the activity is to be seen

Too often the distinction between the church and the world is not sharp enough.

Paul sees it in black and white. He regards the church's environment as depraved.

This is not a popular doctrine. But an army commander has a responsibility to sum up the opposition accurately. It is no less necessary in the spiritual sphere.

The special nature of the activity

The church's mission must concentrate on the word of life. By this Paul means the gospel. It is the church's task to preach this gospel. It must be clearly distinguished from political and social action.

What a depraved world needs is the gospel. It is to be held out so that it shines as light. This requires some kind of public proclamation of it.

Personal interests in the activity

No one was more active for the gospel than Paul. It is not surprising that he looks for the same kind of action in his converts.

It is inconceivable that the work of the dynamic apostle should produce others who do nothing. Paul expects to be able to boast over them at the end.

> *How sad it would have been if Paul had run in vain. What is our expectancy for our church community? Or more pointedly, what is our expectancy for ourselves?*

PHILIPPIANS 2:17, 18
Readiness to offer everything

*Paul is nothing if not wholehearted. His
missionary work is marked by total commitment.*

He shows great concern for the Philippians
His work for them had sprung from a deep affection for
them (cf. Phil. 1:3–11). A martyr spirit results only from a
real concern for others.

He recognises the importance of the truth
Self-sacrifice demands an adequate incentive. To be
poured out for others is desirous only if others will benefit
from it. Paul is spurred on by the Philippians' faith.

He believes such self-giving should promote joy
The sufferings of God's servants move us to tears, but Paul
anticipates a sharing of joy, not sorrow. It has been a
constant paradox that martyrdom of God's servants so
often leads to a deeper joy. Jesus's joy through shame is the
supreme example of joy even in death (Heb. 12:2).

*How much do we share of this total commitment?
Even if we cannot emulate it, we should at least be
inspired by it to be more ready to serve the Lord.*

PHILIPPIANS 2:19–30
Two representative Christian workers

*There is value sometimes in comparing two men of
God. It demonstrates the variety of servants whom
God uses and helps us to appreciate differing but
equally important gifts.*

Timothy, a man of sensitivity

(a) *He was a man close to Paul's heart.* When Paul needs
a messenger he sends Timothy. There was a common
bond of sympathy between them.

(b) *He was concerned about the Philippians.* He seems to
have stood out in this respect.

(c) *He was unselfish in his approach.* As compared with
others, he did not put his own affairs first.

(d) *He had given special service to Paul.* Note the father–
son illustration of the relationship between them.

This man was a gem to have as a fellow-worker.

Epaphroditus, a man of action

(a) *He was the Philippians' representative.* He had come at
their request to look after Paul's needs.

(b) *He was closely linked with Paul's work.* He was a
fellow-worker and fellow-soldier.

(c) *He was concerned because the Philippians were dis-
tressed over his illness.* What affected him, affected
them.

(d) *He had hazarded his life for Paul's sake.* Here was an
activist not concerned about his own safety.

(e) *He wanted to return to Philippi.* On his return there
he deserved to be received with honour.

*Here were two men who both served Paul and the
gospel. According to their different gifts and
abilities, they put the work of God before their
own interests.*

PHILIPPIANS 2:19–24
Timothy, the man of God

Here is a brief cameo of a man who is mentioned several times in the New Testament. The various notes about him repay careful study. This passage concentrates on his relation to Paul.

He was to be given a special task by Paul
Paul is not certain how things will work out, but he expresses his intention.

He was chosen because of his relation to the Philippians
He was acting in their interests.

He also had a special relation to Paul
He was like a son to a father. They had served together in the gospel.

His work was closely affected by Paul's fate
He is to report to others what happens to Paul. Paul is nevertheless hoping to pay the Philippians a visit himself.

In the New Testament there is no finer example of loyal service than is seen in Timothy. He proved to be thoroughly reliable to the apostle.

PHILIPPIANS 2:25–30
Fellow-labourers

This section gives a lesson in co-operation. It concerns the Philippians, Paul and Epaphroditus.

(a) *Paul* had first preached at Philippi.
(b) *The Philippians* had sent gifts to Paul. Epaphroditus had taken these (4:18). He was their minister.

133

(c) *Epaphroditus* had become a fellow-worker with Paul. Paul calls him brother, fellow-worker, fellow-soldier. He had moreover risked his neck for Paul.

(d) *The Philippians* had shown concern over Epaphroditus.

(e) *Epaphroditus* was concerned about the Philippians.

(f) *Paul* is concerned about both.

Such co-operation provides an effective programme for all Christian groups. This is the manifestation of real Christian care.

PHILIPPIANS 2:25–30
Epaphroditus

We know nothing of him except from this epistle. Here is a man who exemplifies several spiritual lessons.

Spiritual quality

He had attained a share in Paul's work which entitles him to be a fellow-worker and fellow-soldier. Clearly Paul highly valued his co-operation.

Tender sympathy

He was concerned about the Philippians. Paul's own concern had prompted a caring attitude on the part of both Epaphroditus and the Philippians. Sympathy tends to engender more sympathy.

Suffering

Epaphroditus comes to an afflicted apostle and becomes caught up in the same affliction. He risked his life for the cause of the gospel.

Mercy

God had mercy on both him and Paul in sparing him. He is always concerned about the welfare of his servants.

Regard

Paul was anxious to encourage true regard among Christians for those working in the service of God. He sees this as a Christian responsibility.

Epaphroditus is a good pattern for anyone who works for God.

PHILIPPIANS 3:1–3
Christian joy and its conditions

Paul never tires of the theme of joy.
He mentions it several times in this letter.
It should be a high priority for all Christians.

Christian joy is in the Lord

It is unlike any other joy because it has a perfect cause and a perfect object. All our joy comes from the Lord, the bringer of deliverance.

The quality of joy is determined by the worthiness of its object. Contrast rejoicing in the Lord with joy over material possessions or human relationships. The Lord is never changing, ever satisfying.

Christian joy is a duty

It can be the subject of a command. Paul makes no allowance for human weakness. There is no consideration over how the readers might feel.

He assumes that all of them ought to rejoice. He was himself a shining example.

Christian joy is a repeatable theme

Paul says it is not irksome to repeat the same things. Great Christian truths are worth repeating.

Those who have experienced the blessings of the gospel never tire of hearing about them.

Christian joy is contrasted with other ways of life
The dogs against which Paul warns his readers are no doubt
Jews who are insisting on circumcision. Their joy is centred
in performing the right ceremonies.

But the Christian puts his confidence in God, not in
religious ceremonies.

Christian joy is a real possibility.
It is independent of circumstances.
It does not rely on human achievement.

PHILIPPIANS 3:1–3
Encouragements and warnings

In the Christian life it is continually necessary to
have a combination of both these things.

The one to rejoice in
Paul knows the answer. Self-centredness is ruled out. The
focus is on the Lord. Since he is constant, joy becomes
stable. This is a theme worthy of constant emphasis.

The people to avoid
Some are opposed to the gospel. This requires alertness –
note the threefold 'look out'. Even religious movements
can sometimes result in the propagation of evil. This is a
sober reminder.

The worship to encourage
Forms and ceremonies are not themselves worship. Paul
stresses the spiritual side. Worship consists in glorying in
Christ. It involves no confidence in the flesh.

Christians must always be on the alert for both
positive and negative purposes. Create the right
impression of joyful Christianity and watch out for
inferior alternatives.

PHILIPPIANS 3:1
Sameness

We are living in an age which is always seeking after new things. Change is regarded as essential to progress. Perhaps Paul's brief statement may provide a caution.

Some sameness is necessary

Much of life is dependent on things being the same. In that way continuity is established.

Paul recognises the need for repetition. Each time we hear spiritual truths we find reinforcement in them.

To some sameness is tedious

Repetition is only irksome when the subject matter ceases to fire our imagination. With Paul this state was never realised in relation to the things of God.

To others sameness is safe

Paul is convinced he must write the same things to the Philippians. It is always safer to underline existing realities than to introduce new and exciting ideas that may lead astray.

Innovation in the things of God is dangerous.

God's revelation does not admit of improvement. Sameness in proclaiming it is therefore a virtue. That gospel has remained the same since first preached.

PHILIPPIANS 3:2, 3
Contemptuous language

It is unusual for Paul to use such language. He must have had strong reason for employing such a term as 'dogs'. Reflect on the uses and dangers of such an approach.

Its use must be regarded as strictly limited
Paul does not hesitate in this case to call people 'dogs'. He does not do this elsewhere, although he does at times criticise wrong ideas in strong terms. In this case he considered his opponents to be worthy of such language.

Contemptuous language can rebound on the user
In this case the Jews were receiving some of their own medicine. They were in the habit of calling the Gentiles 'dogs'. They could not complain when the same term was applied to them. Such rebounds are not uncommon.

The language here is directed against evil workers
Perhaps Paul was wanting to shock the Philippians into recognising the true character of these Judaisers.

While contemptuous language is generally dangerous, especially in Christian contexts, there are rare occasions where it is justified.

PHILIPPIANS 3:4–11
The example of Paul

This section is one of Paul's biographical passages. It throws some interesting light on his background and his attitude towards it.

His renunciations
The list of his Jewish privileges is given to emphasise what he was prepared to give up for Christ.

(a) He was a fully accredited Jew.
(b) He was from an honoured tribe – a thoroughgoing Hebrew.
(c) He was particularly religious – a Pharisee.
(d) He had proved his religious convictions by persecuting Christians.

To the Jews he was thoroughly respectable and esteemed. Yet he gave up all his inherited and developed privileges. He even regarded them as refuse.

His quest for knowledge

He sees life as in a balance – with the gains outweighing the losses. He seeks knowledge of Christ as Lord.

It is a personal quest – highly individual. It is an excellent quest – he speaks of its surpassing worth. He sees it as the most precious pursuit – everything else loses value by comparison.

His quest for righteousness

This had long occupied his mind. Under Pharisaism he pronounced himself blameless under the law.

It was a satisfying achievement. But he came to discover that it was a righteousness of his own. This he had to reject to find a better. To be found in Christ brought a righteousness from God through faith.

The righteousness he found was no longer self-satisfying, but Christ-centred. His own efforts were given up in order to gain Christ (cf. the parable of the pearl of great price).

His anticipations

(a) Knowledge of Christ is always progressive. The quest is never finished in this life. 'That I may know him' must be every Christian's quest.
(b) But Paul adds another target – the power of his resurrection. He sees Christ's resurrection as his energy source.
(c) Sharing his sufferings. Paul had already had his share of this, but does not ask for easement. He sees the possibility of suffering until his dying day. He finds inspiration in Christ's example.
(d) Attaining the resurrection from the dead. This is

every believer's goal. It involves the transformation of the existing body.

The example of Paul is undoubtedly pitched high. The total commitment may seem too demanding for lesser mortals. But Paul would consider nothing less worthwhile.

PHILIPPIANS 3:4–7
A Christian's estimate of privilege

In secular life privileges are important, but often evoke distrust and envy. Religions built on privilege are bound to promote division. Paul had to reassess his own values.

Repudiation of external rites
To a Jew circumcision was important. But every culture has a certain amount of ritual on which its people depend.

Repudiation of pedigree
Paul's pedigree was impeccable. The right nation – Israel. The right tribe – Benjamin. The right culture – Hebrew.

The Jews of Jesus' day were proud of being Abraham's sons. But pedigree means nothing in Christian terms. No one can claim any advantage.

Repudiation of religious status
Pharisees had much to be said for them. They achieved much for Judaism. But they had developed a superiority approach.

In their own society the Pharisees stood above the common people. They illustrate the wrong values of all class systems.

Repudiation of undiscriminating zeal

There is something attractive about all forms of enthusiasm, none more so than religious zeal. But history is full of atrocities perpetrated through religious zeal. Consider the Inquisition.

Paul was a religious bigot before his conversion. He never forgot his wrongly placed enthusiasm.

Repudiation of pride in religious blamelessness

Paul really believed in his blamelessness. He thought of himself as better than others.

This is one of the hardest of all privilege claims to reassess. It requires a high measure of humility.

A Christian is a person who has come to God without any privileges. All rights must be renounced and the sinner's role totally acknowledged.

PHILIPPIANS 3:7, 8
A Christian profit and loss account

The natural way of assessing values has to be totally transformed. We must estimate using new standards.

Previous advantages may become present hindrances

Non-Christians esteem many things as valuable. But for Paul these have become positive obstacles. He speaks of what was profitable to him.

Advantages without Christ have no lasting value

Those advantages previously treasured by Paul had now become worthless in the light of Christian truth. Everything had become loss.

Rejection of advantages is worthwhile to gain Christ
Paul speaks of the surpassing worth of Christ.

The Christian equation is: Give up advantages
and gain Christ. This way you gain everything.
When the profit margin is worked out, it is
immense.

PHILIPPIANS 3:8, 9
The knowledge of Christ

Paul sees knowledge of Christ as the greatest
possible treasure. The more we know the more we
value what we know.

What it means
Paul refers to 'Christ Jesus my Lord'. Knowing Christ is
knowing the gospel. It encompasses all that God in Christ
has done for us.

How it may be obtained
Everything cherished must be considered loss. Paul even
describes these things as rubbish. Only those who have
experienced Christ have begun to acquire such knowledge.

What it will lead to
Paul talks about being 'found in him'. This brings great
security, for nothing can touch us in him. It virtually means
we sink ourselves in him.

What we shall gain from it.
Knowledge will point to righteousness. To be in him means
that his righteousness becomes ours. God looks at us as
believers 'in Christ'.

This is a specialist kind of knowledge
But it is available to all who exercise faith.

PHILIPPIANS 3:10, 11
Getting to know Christ

The quest for knowledge makes demands,
especially when the subject of knowing is Christ.
Paul gives us some of the implications.

Paul's resolve
'I want to know Christ.' There is determination in the statement. It does not happen accidentally.

It requires effort and discipline. This knowledge is more than knowing about Christ. There is a yearning here for closer acquaintance.

Paul's pursuit of power
Knowing Christ involves a quest for a different kind of power. It is not personal ambition, but the same kind of power which raised Jesus from the dead.

Paul's willingness to suffer
Paul is eager to share the sufferings of Christ. He has already known much of this. It shows his dedication to the cause of Christ.

Paul's anticipation of the resurrection
Knowing Christ has a future aspect. This is the believer's destiny. Here Paul must be thinking of the transformation of the body which he mentions in 3:21. Knowing Christ means becoming like him.

All should profit from reflection on Paul's quest,
since the same quest should be the target of
every Christian.

PHILIPPIANS 3:10
Sharing suffering with Christ

*Christians have their own approach to suffering.
They learn to see it as part of God's purpose. But
Paul's theme of suffering with Christ is something
different.*

All Christians may have to suffer with Christ

Paul's Christian confession at once placed him at variance
with his environment. Proclamation of the gospel challenged the *status quo*.

Jesus predicted persecution and the early Christians
suffered opposition from Jews and Gentiles alike. To identify with Christ means sharing his reproach.

Suffering with Christ has many forms

A glance at 2 Cor. 11:23–29 will show the variety of Paul's
sufferings. He concentrates on the physical aspects. But he
also suffered from mental and social pressures.

Some suffering is barbarous; other types more sophisti-
cated. Whatever the form, suffering *for* Christ is to be seen
as suffering *with* Christ.

Suffering with Christ is seen as a privilege

Paul actually wants to know this. His standard is to be like
Christ in his death. How can anyone welcome such painful
experiences? Only because love for Christ sees such suffering as an honour.

Note that suffering has a preservative function. It roots
out corruption and mere profession.

*If Christians are called to carry their cross as Christ
carried his, they are also assured of sharing his
glory.*

PHILIPPIANS 3:12–16
Pressing towards the goal

*Paul's view of ongoing Christian life is a pattern
for us all. He was never satisfied.*

Recognising the imperfect

There is no hope for those who think they are perfect. If the
apostle realises acutely his present limitations, should any
lesser mortal ever be satisfied?

True spiritual progress rests on restlessness over present
achievement.

Pressing on to perfection

Why bother, if it is unattainable? Why not be satisfied with
a lower standard? Paul's answer is that Christ Jesus has
made him his own.

This means that Christ's satisfaction with us is more
important than our satisfaction with ourselves. Paul knows
he has not yet arrived.

Forgetting the past

Paul was determined not to be dominated by the past.
Contrast with those who live on former glories, or those
who can never forget former failures.

Christian living demands forgetting as much as re-
membering. The present is more important than the past.

Keeping on target

The successful know where they are going. The expert
archer sees the bull's-eye. It is essential to define the
goal – Paul calls it the prize of the upward call of God in
Christ.

He sees the future prize as infinitely more valuable than
anything in his past experience.

Following an example

Paul assumes that all mature Christians should adopt the
same pattern of progress. He even assumes that God will
make it clear to those who think otherwise.

It is a sobering thought that lack of dissatisfaction with

spiritual achievement is the measure of a person's maturity. This rules out all complacency and smugness.

Paul could not have set before us a higher goal. His intention is that we should face the challenge, not turn away from it in despair.

PHILIPPIANS 3:12–16
The value of forgetfulness

Most people regard forgetfulness as a limitation, but there are positive advantages. It would be intolerable if we could never forget. Paul develops this in a spiritual way.

Memory often fastens on past failures
We more easily recall unpleasant experiences.

Memory can make us complacent over past successes
We cannot continually exist on past resources.

Forgetting helps us concentrate on present challenges
Those absorbed in the past do not see clearly the needs of the present.

We could not live without memory. It preserves God's wonderful dealings with us. There is much that we must remember, but we are called to forget our former failures or successes.

PHILIPPIANS 3:12–14
Progressive Christianity

There are spiritual laws which govern progress.
These are illustrated in this passage.

A dissatisfaction with the present
The basis of dissatisfaction is Paul's awareness of not having made his own what Christ has already made his.

The dissatisfaction is not with Christ, but with our own appropriation of Christ.

A selective approach to the past
Putting the past behind clears the way ahead. Paul is thinking in strategic terms. The 'we have always done it this way' mentality finds no support from Paul.

The apostle is certainly not meaning to suggest that the past can teach us nothing.

An ambitious approach to the future
There are more spiritual fields to conquer. But it requires determined effort (note the idea of straining forward).

The goal and prize are intended to spur us on.

All living is controlled by past, present and future.
The mature Christian must get the balance right.

PHILIPPIANS 3:15, 16
Unity and maturity

Paul has talked of unity in 1:27–2:4. But here he
links it with maturity.

Unity of mind is a desirable aim
Paul's standards are set high. But he assumes that all can have the same aims. Consider the effect if all Christians

were striving for the same gaol – not for their own ambitions, but for the upward call of God.

High spiritual levels are dynamic. Are we in line with others because our aims are too small? Or are we out of line because we think we are more perfect then we are?

Where unity of mind is lacking, rely on God

Here is a valuable lesson. Othermindedness often leads to dissensions. But God desires all to have high aims.

Paul is ready to leave the education process to God. The demand is comprehensive – 'if in anything'. Nothing must lessen the high target.

Unity of mind demands consistency

Mature Christians hold on to what they have attained. Does this not conflict with Paul's turning his back on what lies behind?

Unity can never exist among those whose grasp of truth is always changing, or whose ideas are so fluid that no oneness with others can be attained.

Spiritual maturity does not just happen.
It requires effort and tenacity.
We should make it our constant aim.

PHILIPPIANS 3:17–21
Citizens of heaven

Paul sees his own approach as an example for the readers to imitate. This leads him to contrast the opposing forms of citizenship. He may have been influenced by the fact that Philippi as a colony could claim Roman citizenship.

A warning about the wrong kind of citizens

(a) *They live as enemies of the cross of Christ.* It is the attitude of people towards the cross which determines citizenship. There is no other test. Those opposed to or even indifferent to the cross are citizens of earth.

(b) *They live to gratify their fleshly desires.* Paul puts it strongly. These people have as their god their belly. This sums up the sensual approach to life.

Modern secularised society is increasingly dominated by self-gratification. Western society largely overeats, is ruled by lust, sex, money, materialism. Things become gods. This is the sort of environment in which Christians are living.

(c) *They are morally shameless.* Such attitudes are not confined to Paul's time. Shame over immodesty, immorality or selfish ways of life has vanished. In its place is boasting about freedom and over the banishment of fixed moral values.

Contrast this attitude of glorying in shame with Christ who turned the shame of the cross into glory.

(d) *They think in an earthly way.* People act as they think. Their intellectual climate will reveal their citizenship. They make no room for spiritual realities.

Everything revolves around this life. Paul has only one word for the destiny of such people – destruction.

An encouragement about the right kind of citizenship

(a) *The Christian's citizenship.* The idea of heavenly citizenship is in strong contrast. What does it mean? Is it other-worldliness? Only partially. It stresses where we really belong. The present life is seen as transitory.

(b) *The Christian citizen looks for Christ's coming.* This is a glorious hope which must govern present behaviour. We already have salvation, but there is more to come.

(c) *The Christian citizen knows he will be changed.* At the moment he has to be content with a lowly body. But he is assured of transformation. He can look forward to no less than a body like Christ's glorious body.

Here is a striking contrast to Paul's metaphor of belly-worshippers for the surrounding world. The necessary change will be accomplished by a totally adequate power.

Christians are heavenly citizens in an earthly environment. They are a people apart – strangers and exiles. This should lead them constantly to examine themselves lest they unconsciously adopt the standards of the citizens of this world.

PHILIPPIANS 3:17
Imitation

Imitations or reproductions are often thought of as being inferior when compared with the original. But in the New Testament imitation is encouraged. In this letter Paul has already urged imitation of Christ. Now he urges imitation of himself.

Mature Christians must act as examples to others
Paul knew the value of imitation at a time when Christians had no other ways of knowing how to live and act. He had had much experience. God's hand had been on him. He provided a fine example.

It was not arrogance which led Paul to invite others to imitate him. He was too deeply aware of God's rich mercy towards him. Those who know much of God must always desire that others should emulate their experience.

Christians should note those who live as patterns
Paul seems to be saying: first look at me, then at others who are following the same rules.

Christian leaders have a great responsibility to act in a way that is worth following. Paul's reference to the enemies of the cross vividly contrasts with worthy Christian examples.

History is full of examples of good Christian people. Modern life can provide many worthy parallels. Imitation can be a spur to greater achievement.

PHILIPPIANS 3:18, 19
Enemies of the cross

In any campaign it is essential to know the enemy. Ignorance can lead to most damaging compromise or downright failure.

The need to define the opposition

Paul is not here concerned about opposition to himself. The work of God does not depend on personalities. The opposition was against Christ. Not only so, it was against the cross.

Paul sees antagonism towards the cross as opposition to the core of the gospel. Paul would have had no time for those who water down the gospel of the cross.

The need to recognise their behaviour patterns

The cross means self-denial. Its enemies believe in self-indulgence. The cross challenges the accepted conventions of the age.

No true followers of the cross can make a god of their belly. Watch how people live – whether they can recognise their own shame – and you will know whether they are enemies of the cross or not.

The need to analyse their thought patterns

The cross points to high-mindedness, to the noblest thought patterns ever known. Christ did not please himself. The enemies' thought is earthly minded as if the advantages of this life were all important.

Let us not shirk the responsibility of locating the enemy. The better we know him, the better we shall overcome his opposition.

PHILIPPIANS 4:1–7
Exhortations

For Paul Christianity was always practical. Even after some of his profound theological statements, he comes to practical applications. So often theology and practice have been divorced. But neither flourishes under such separation. In this passage the outworkings are varied.

Unity among fellow-workers

(a) *Paul addresses his readers in an affectionate way.* He calls them brothers, joy and crown, and beloved. His warmth spills over. Those he exhorts are those for whom he has a high regard.

(b) *He addresses some by name.* Euodia and Syntyche are two women who do not agree. Paul uses strong pleas. He desires a common mind in the Lord.

(c) *He addresses another as 'yoke-fellow'.* There is no indication of identity. He is called on to help the women. He was evidently a peace-maker.

(d) *He recognises many fellow-workers.* He includes the women, the yoke-fellow, Clement and the rest whose names are in the book of life. This is all-inclusive. Paul sees the need for co-operation and harmony in the cause of the gospel.

Joy

This is a favourite theme in this letter. Here Paul draws attention to two features – always and again.

When he says always, does this exclude sorrowful experiences which all are subject to? Since he is himself in prison, he is clearly making no exceptions. When he says it again, he is underlining its importance.

Gentleness

This word suggests a reluctance to insist on one's rights. Anyone who acts like this will soon be the object of attention.

In 2 Cor. 10:1 the same word is applied to Christ. A spur to right conduct is the expectation of the return of Christ.

Contentment

Anxiety destroys peace. Paul is very demanding here – no anxiety at all. But how can it be avoided? Paul gives two lines of approach

(a) *Thanksgiving*. Paul puts this before petition.

(b) *Prayer*. This means leaving anxieties with the Lord. The result is God's peace, which Paul says is beyond understanding. It stands like a sentry on guard over feeling and thought. It keeps out what will disturb the equilibrium.

> *These exhortations are not disconnected. They together form the basis for true Christian citizenship.*

PHILIPPIANS 4:1–3
A pastor's concern for his people

> *The pattern which Paul provides is one which all with pastoral concerns might profitably follow.*

A strong bond of fellowship

Paul's relationship to the readers was strongly personal.

Whom I love and long for. There is intensity of feeling here. This shows a complete absence of professionalism. Christian love promotes a strong bond between people.

My joy and crown. He sees his converts as enhancing his mission. He regards them not as jewels in a crown, but as the crown itself.

A strong plea for unity

Agreement in the Lord should be normal. Where it is lacking, as with Euodia and Syntyche, it causes grief.

Paul arranges help from someone else (the true yoke-fellow). Harmony does not happen automatically. It needs prompting.

A strong appreciation of others

Paul acknowledges many fellow-workers. 'Side by side with me' shows that he regards them as equal.

The uniting factor is the gospel. Paul mentions that all of them are recorded in the book of life. The true pastor sees his people with him in the work.

The secret here is concern for 'others' rather than for 'self'.

PHILIPPIANS 4:1
Steadfastness

Here is a much-needed quality. It is essential for the dependability of God's people. It ensures continuity.

It is regarded as a duty

Paul does not argue for its desirability. He does not present it as an option. He sees it as a constant requirement.

It has its basis in the Lord

There is no place for self-dependence or reliance on others. To stand fast we need a firm foundation. Since the Lord does not change, he provides the surest basis.

It results from our citizenship

'Therefore' connects with the end of Chapter 3. Our privileged status carries with it responsibilities. Heavenly citizens must be consistent.

It is pressed home through concern

Paul shows great affection for his brethren. This provides the motive for his appeal to them.

> *Steadfastness is non-glamorous, but no one can do without it. It is more valuable than a ceaseless quest for something new.*

PHILIPPIANS 4:2, 3
Two women and the gospel

> *Philippi was noted in Paul's day for its liberal approach to women. Many held influential positions in society. This was in strong contrast to the widespread view that women were inferior to men.*

Women were highly regarded in the Philippian church

The first Philippian Christian was a woman, Lydia. The first meeting at which the apostle preached was composed of women (Acts 16:13). The first to give the Christian missionaries hospitality was a woman. It is possible that the preponderance of women may account for the generosity of the Philippians.

Euodia and Syntyche were evidently leading members

No details are given of their position. But it is significant that they are named, since few others are so mentioned in this epistle. They had worked side by side with Paul.

Their influence was marred through disagreement

It should be noted that women are not more prone to disharmony than men, for in 2:2 Paul addresses the whole church in a similar way. Whatever the reason for the disharmony, whether difference of method, temperament or rivalry, it caused concern.

Their names are recorded in the book of life
They are as important as Clement and others who are
unnamed. The true yoke-fellow is called on to help. We
know nothing of him apart from his evident skill in patching
up quarrels.

It is a pity that disharmony marred these women,
but they were nevertheless valuable members of the
community. They would have been more helpful if
they had learned to agree.

PHILIPPIANS 4:4–7
Christian joy

Many things bring joy into everyday life. But
Christian joy, while allied to this, is of a superior
kind.

Joy is a requirement for the Christian
It is not a matter of temperament, but of obligation. It is
part of the definition of a Christian (cf. Gal. 5:22). It is
needed even in adverse circumstances, as Paul found out in
prison.

Joy must be in the Lord
We can rejoice in what the Lord is and in what he has done.
But more than that, we who are in the Lord share the joy of
the Lord.

Joy is linked with gentleness and forbearance
Joy is not an isolated experience. Christians must get their
priorities right, especially in view of the Lord's coming.

Joy dispels anxiety
Paul insists on thanksgiving with prayer. The joyful Christian commits everything to God. Paul is a great example
here.

Joy and peace go together.
Both are part of the fruit of the Spirit (Gal. 5:22). Real peace is beyond description. It can only be experienced. It affects both emotions (heart) and intellect (mind).

The wonder is that there is not more Christian joy around.

PHILIPPIANS 4:4
The Christian duty of rejoicing

It may seem strange to talk of duty and rejoicing together. But joy is no arduous duty.

Why should Christians rejoice?
  (a) Because it is commanded.
  (b) Because it is prompted by the Spirit (Gal. 5:22).

What should they rejoice in?
The content of the joy is the Lord.
  The joy will never dry up when they meditate on him.

How often should they rejoice?
Always. Is this possible? What happens when sorrow comes? See 2 Cor. 6:10.

Why is the command repeated?
This shows its importance. Paul mentions his own joy in 1:4 and exhorts his readers in 3:1. He still thinks it necessary to repeat it again here.

Let us use the above questions to assess the value we place on rejoicing.

PHILIPPIANS 4:6, 7
Anxiety and its antidote

Most people are affected by worry. Some think it to be a matter of disposition. It is supposed that some are worriers and others are not. But Paul makes no allowance for disposition. He puts an embargo on anxiety.

Is anxiety ever legitimate?
Does Paul really rule it out completely? We should distinguish between anxiety and care. It is not wrong to have concern, but anxiety shows a lack of confidence in God.

Is prayer an effective antidote?
It is as comprehensive as the subject of anxiety – i.e. it includes everything. It means sharing all our cares. Prayer itself is varied. Note the variety of words Paul uses – prayer, supplication and thanksgiving.

Is it possible always to be at peace?
Calmness and serenity are much admired qualities. But are they beyond our reach? The peace Paul mentions is no ordinary peace. It is what God gives, it baffles analysis and it stands guard over our hearts.

When God's peace takes possession, anxieties fade. The antidote really works.

PHILIPPIANS 4:8, 9
Meditation and action

Since thought affects action, it is important to meditate in order to clarify the thoughts.

The value of meditation

Paul assumes as axiomatic that Christians will think. Thoughtless Christians can never be relied on for right action. Paul places great store on the mind.

He can speak of the need for mind renewal (Rom. 12:2). Christians have to re-educate their thoughts to think in a Christian way.

The subjects for meditation

Paul gives a remarkable list. What is true, honourable, just, pure, lovely, gracious, excellent – these are demanding standards.

They are pre-eminently found in God's revelation to man. But not exclusively so. The implication is that whatever does not fit into these categories is not suitable food for Christian meditation.

The example for action

Paul has no time for mere dreamers or idle thinkers. He points the way to action.

What is learned, received, heard, seen, must be done. Consider the power of example in translating any thought into action.

The reward of thoughtful action

When thought is right, action will be right and peace will follow. Note the repetition from verse 7.

The proverb 'Think before you act' is prudent advice for anyone, but it is imperative for the Christian.

PHILIPPIANS 4:8
Thinking about our thinking

Some think very little. Few think profoundly.
Fewer still think about the quality of their thought.
Paul is urging such an exercise from a Christian
point of view.

Absolute subjects
Truth has become too relative. There is an absolute standard for gauging what is true (i.e. God's word). Love of truth raises Christian integrity. What is honourable is never merely relative.

Relative subjects
Paul lists several examples.
  (a) *What is just.* This applies to human relationships.
  (b) *What is pure.* Mental purity leads to purity of action. This is essential in the modern environment of impurity.
  (c) *What is lovely.* This indicates a nature which leads to an attractive character. Christian character should be beautiful.
  (d) *What is gracious.* This points to a personality that speaks well of others.

This list is demanding. *Excellence* and *worthy of praise* sum up the list in more general terms.

Clearly, positive action is necessary. The mind
needs discipline to ensure the right kind of thought.
Nothing but good can result from improving the
quality of our thinking.

PHILIPPIANS 4:9
Christian example

When Paul appeals to his own example, he is the pattern for all Christians. Taken out of context his approach may seem arrogant (cf. 3:17). Nevertheless example can be a powerful agency for good.

The apostle's message
'What you have learned and received.' What did this involve? The preaching of the gospel and all its practical implications.

The apostle's example
'What you have heard and seen in me.' This is an echo of 1:30. The readers knew something of what Paul had gone through. It must have been a real inspiration when the Philippians found themselves hard pressed.

The apostle's assurance
He is convinced that the God of peace would be with others, because he had experienced that peace himself.

We have a message to proclaim, an example to show and an assurance to give. We should remember the power of an effective pattern.

PHILIPPIANS 4:10–20
Gratitude for material help

Matters of money in human relationships are always delicate. Paul provides an example of how to maintain a right balance between independence and appreciation of the help of others.

Concern

The Philippians were interested in Paul's affairs. Concern should be the hallmark of all Christians.

   (a) Paul rejoices over their concern. Note the intensity of this kind of joy.

   (b) He recognises that concern was present even when no opportunity to contribute existed. Presumably their resources would not stretch to it.

Contentment

Paul does not complain of want. Want is something created when expectation exceeds reality. Paul gives the antidote.

   (a) Contentment is a settled state. This can exist in 'whatsoever state'. This is a fool-proof situation, for nothing can disturb it. It should be noted that this does not automatically happen – it has to be learned.

   (b) Contentment can exist in contrasting situations. Abased – abounding; plenty – hunger; abundance – want. These are extreme contrasts but true contentment is resilient to stand such changes.

Paul's fast changing circumstances made great demands on his sense of contentment.

Conviction

Such resilient contentment demands an explanation. Paul's source of strength is Christ. He is convinced of his ability.

   (a) Paul's past experience has depended on Christ. His conversion and missionary call testify to that.

   (b) He is convinced that strength is available in all circumstances. His understanding of all things is conditioned by his whole-hearted commitment to

Christ. 'All things' in Christ's service merit Christ's strength.

Contribution

See what Paul says about the help the Philippians had sent.
  (a) It was an act of kindness.
  (b) It was not an isolated act.
  (c) The significance was more important than the gift.
  (d) It was a fragrant offering.
  (e) It was pleasing to God.

Conclusion

God is no man's debtor. Those who contribute may be sure that God will meet their needs (to be distinguished from wants). No wonder Paul ends with a doxology.

Although this passage deals with a specific situation, the principles it brings out are timeless.

PHILIPPIANS 4:10–13
The secret of contentment

This passage shows the powerful example of Paul. If ever a man had learned to be content it was he.

An example of rejoicing
  (a) No one more keenly appreciated the kindness of others.
  (b) No one more readily detected the grace of God behind the material support he received.

An example of contentment

The apostle shows from his own experience that contentment is possible. 'Whatever the circumstances' for him covered a massive list of hardships (cf. 2 Cor. 11).

An example of inner strength

Paul's resources are open to all Christians. The key is the

strength which Christ supplies. How did this strength come to Paul?

   (a) Through Christ's example.
   (b) Through his teaching.
   (c) Through the gift of the Spirit.

With such rich resources it is possible for all Christians to experience the same contentment. We need to examine ourselves to discover how much of it we display.

PHILIPPIANS 4:12, 13
The problems of prosperity

The prosperous are seldom aware of the dangers. The underprivileged cannot even conceive of them. But Paul had arrived at a remarkably balanced position.

We need a view of wealth which holds good in adversity

Paul's circumstances were constantly fluctuating. But his approach to success remained unaffected.

We need a view of success which does not spoil us

Those who know how to be abased can be trusted with abounding.

Material resources must never be an end in themselves. True contentment can exist only when it is independent of circumstances.

PHILIPPIANS 4:13
Christian strength

Most are conscious of weakness. There is a general desire to be stronger Christians. For this reason Paul's words on this theme are particularly relevant.

Christians are meant to be strong
Paul has a positive approach to life. For him there is no such word as 'can't'.

Christians have an unfailing source of strength
Paul had learned not to rely on his own strength. In Christ, he drew from Christ's power working in him.

Christians can experience strength for all occasions
Paul faced hardships, but remained positive (1 Cor. 4:8ff.; 2 Cor. 11:23ff.). He faced many difficulties in his work. But he triumphed through Christ.

If Christians are meant to be strong, weakness is inexcusable. It reflects adversely on our resources in Christ.

PHILIPPIANS 4:14–18
Liberality

Gifts are a tangible expression of affection. Here Paul interprets the gifts given by the Philippians towards his needs. The motive behind the gifts is always more important than the gifts themselves.

Liberality is more than almsgiving
Almsgiving can be impersonal and can proceed from duty. But the Philippians' liberality went beyond this. It was proof of their Christian concern and love.

Liberality calls for gracious acceptance
Paul did not want to ask for gifts. He often claimed independence (1 Thess. 2:5; 2 Thess. 3:8). Yet in this case he graciously received the gifts.

Liberality must not lead to covetousness
Paul is anxious to dispel any suggestion that he valued the gifts more highly than the giver.

Liberality is a fragrant exercise
It is like a sweet odour to other people and is pleasing to God.

The Christian attitude reflects the amazing generosity of God.

PHILIPPIANS 4:19
Ample resources

In responding to the readers' generosity, Paul makes a reassuring statement about God's provision.

We all have needs that God alone can meet
(a) Material needs. Most people think that they must fend for themselves. But the Christian should learn to trust God for material needs. It is only he who really knows the nature of our needs.
(b) Spiritual needs. No one can ever become self-sufficient. We need forgiveness, restoration, strength, and spiritual knowledge.

God promises to supply our need
God's resources are limitless. No crisis can arise as a result of God's inability. But we must note that his way of meeting our needs will almost certainly differ from the way we have imagined.

The resources are made available in Christ

God's promises are limited to those who are in Christ. That is the link with the source of supply. To know Christ is to know God's riches. To know him is to share God's glory.

It seems too good to be true, until we realise that such resources impose great responsibilities. A poverty-stricken Christian should be a contradiction in terms.

PHILIPPIANS 4:21–23
Salutations

Greetings have value in cementing human relationships. We should not neglect this way of expressing goodwill.

Greetings from Paul

Christian greetings can be much more meaningful than general greetings because of the deep bond which exists between Christians.

   (a) Greeting is an expression of Christian courtesy.

   (b) Greeting is here extended to every saint. Paul has no intention of being selective.

This reflects his warm approach to his readers.

Greetings from others

It is a great joy when others can join us in greeting.

   (a) *The brethren*. These are anonymous. But the warmth of their fellowship shines through. Even unknown Christians can share greetings in a meaningful way.

   (b) *Those in Caesar's household*. These were probably in the Emperor's employment. Their status is unknown, but their environment can be deduced. Since the Caesar was the infamous Nero, we can only begin to imagine the problems. But the greetings of these people are valued.

After the greeting came the usual benediction. We can only surmise the effect of the letter on the original readers. We can then perhaps discern somewhat more precisely its effect on ourselves.

COLOSSIANS
Introduction

About Colossae
Colossae was a small city in the Lycus valley in the Roman province of Asia. It was a near neighbour of Laodicea and Hieropolis, both of which overshadowed it in importance. Paul had never been there but had been kept informed about the church by Epaphras, one of the members.

About the church
We have no specific knowledge about its origin. The most likely suggestion is that Epaphras, who was acquainted with Paul, commenced a Christian witness in his own city of Colossae. It seems that at an early stage in its development certain people were teaching wrong ideas about the Christian faith, an inadequate idea of Christ, and an overstress on ritual requirements (circumcision, food and feast days). Epaphras is sent to obtain advice from Paul.

About the purpose of the letter
Following reports about the false teaching, Paul writes his letter to exhort his readers towards a higher view of Christ and of his demands on them for a worthy manner of living. Unlike most of his epistles, this one includes greetings from several people who are personally named.

About the writer
This is another of the letters written by Paul the prisoner. Since he refers to Onesimus, Mark, Aristarchus, Demas and Luke, in addition to Epaphras in both Colossians and Philemon, it is clear that these two epistles were written at the same time. Both Epaphras and Onesimus are being sent

back to Colossae with Paul's letters. Paul also seems to have sent at the same time a letter to the Laodiceans (Col. 4:16), which has not been preserved.

About the date

Since Paul is a prisoner, most scholars would date this letter at some time during his Roman imprisonment. It is not possible to be certain about the precise date, but Paul is evidently on trial for his life. Some have proposed a date during a suggested Ephesian imprisonment of Paul, which would place it five to six years earlier. It seems reasonable to suppose that Colossians and Ephesians were written about the same time, because many ideas occur in both. A.D. 60 might be a likely date.

COLOSSIANS 1:1–14
A message to an unknown group

Paul writes to a church he had never visited. He depends on what he has heard from others.

Greeting

(a) *It is sent from*
1. Paul, described as an apostle of Jesus Christ. He is conscious that this is by God's choice.
2. Timothy, our brother. He is similarly linked in 2 Cor., Phil., and 1 and 2 Thess.

(b) *It is sent to* the saints at Colossae. Note how Paul classes all Christians as saints.

(c) *It consists of* grace and peace, after Paul's normal pattern.

Thanksgiving

Paul and Timothy are agreed about giving thanks.

(a) *To whom given.* To God the Father of our Lord Jesus Christ.

(b) *On what founded.* Paul has heard of their faith and love. Clearly the Colossians have established a strong Christian tradition and witness. Paul recognises that the faith and love spring from hope. Their minds were conditioned by the future.

(c) *For what content.* Paul is specially thankful for the fruitfulness of the gospel seen in them. This is characteristic of the gospel. Fruitfulness follows from an understanding of the grace of God.

(d) *For what particular person.* Although all are included, Epaphras is singled out.

He is
> our beloved fellow servant,
> a faithful minister,
> a spiritually minded reporter.

Prayer

It is Paul's practice to link prayer with thanksgiving. This consists of two main sections.

(a) *For increased knowledge.* Christian faith is progressive. There is always more to know. Paul speaks of
> knowledge,
> spiritual wisdom,
> understanding.

All these are mental aspects.

(b) *For a developed character.* Knowledge alone is not enough. There must be a practical outcome. Here is a prayer for
> worthy living,
> increasing strength,
> a share in the inheritance,
> a recognition of forgiveness.

There is a strong sense of confidence in Paul's greeting, thanksgiving and prayer.

COLOSSIANS 1:1, 2
An apostle sends his greetings

All Paul's salutations are similar, but each has its salient points. Here we may ask three questions.

What does it tell us about the apostle?

(a) His consciousness of his divinely appointed office.

(b) His willingness to regard Timothy as a brother and to include him in the greeting.

What does it tell us about the readers?

(a) They formed the church at Colossae, a small town in the Lycus valley.

(b) They are called 'saints' in the sense that all Christians are set apart for a holy purpose.

(c) They are described as faithful brethren. They had been true to the gospel.

What does it tell us about Paul's desire for them?
His greeting here is the common one of grace and peace.

(a) Grace points especially to God's grace.

(b) Peace is clearly the peace which comes from God.

This greeting will be seen to be wholly God-centred. What better opening could there be for a Christian letter!

COLOSSIANS 1:3–8
Thanks for what God is doing

Whenever we hear of God's activity it should lead to praise. Our praise should not be restricted to the activity in which we have ourselves been involved. Praise should always be outward looking.

The Christians had heard the word
Paul calls the gospel the word of truth. Hearing the word is the first stage towards faith.

The Christians had believed in Christ
They had responded to the gospel. Whenever and wherever people believe, it is a cause of great thanksgiving.

The Christians had shown love to others
Not only had they recognised the need for brotherly love, but they extended it to Christians everywhere.

The Christians had become fruitful
This means that they had developed and shown many Christian graces. Cf. Gal. 5:22 for Paul's idea of fruitfulness.

The Christians had gained a hope for the future
They had acquired an understanding of where they were
going. Future destiny has some significance for present action.

*Paul does not omit to name his source of
information. His knowledge, though second-hand,
is thoroughly reliable. It was from a fellow-servant
and faithful minister. Paul was able to rejoice
together with all concerned.*

COLOSSIANS 1:6
The productiveness of the gospel

*Paul is convinced that the gospel is actively at
work. Consider his statement here.*

The gospel bears fruit
Clearly Paul is thinking of the good influence of the gospel.
It bears fruit in the people who respond to it. This is a highly
personal effectiveness.

The fruit is seen in the world
Paul is always outward looking. The church is a community
which should affect the world. This means that the spiritual
fruit must be produced in an adverse environment.

The fruit can affect the whole world
It is not dependent on a particular culture or stratum of
society. It is universal. It is recognisable anywhere.

The fruit proceeds from God's grace
There is a mystery here. The fruitfulness of the gospel is not
due to man's effort, but to God's sovereign operation.

*It will be seen that the gospel is not just a creed
which we believe. It is a dynamic force which
produces dramatic effects in our lives.*

COLOSSIANS 1:9–14
Paul's prayer

*In his prayers Paul often uses expressions of
fullness. He does so here. Note the expressions,
'we have not ceased to pray', and 'that you may be
filled'. The apostle shows a thorough-going
approach.*

Fullness of knowledge

All would agree that this is a worthy aim. People in all ages
have sought knowledge. The Stoic aim was 'Know thyself'.

Paul's vision is wider – knowledge of God's will. This
covers everything of relevance to the Christian. Spiritual
wisdom and understanding are aspects of the all-inclusive
knowledge.

Fullness of power

Link power with knowledge and the combination is un-
stoppable. Again Paul is comprehensive – all power, endurance, patience. The measure is God's glorious might.

But for what purpose is this knowledge and power?

(a) To lead a worthy life.

(b) To thank God for our inheritance, deliverance and
redemption.

*All Christians are expected to possess knowledge
and power. If we are conscious of our weakness,
we need the kind of prayer that Paul prayed.*

COLOSSIANS 1:9, 10
Getting to know God's will

No Christian is ever exempt from such a quest.
There is a constant need to examine ourselves to
discover whether what we are doing is according to
what God wants of us.

Its importance
Paul does not cease to pray for this for his readers. It is
noticeable that he does not here pray for knowledge of
God, although this is important, but more specifically for
knowledge of God's will.

Its means
In answer to the question, How do we know God's will?
Paul suggests,
   (a) that it can be known;
   (b) that it can be attained through spiritual wisdom.
This sets it apart from human wisdom.

Its results
God's will is directed to practical needs. It should lead to
worthy living and fruit bearing. If these are absent, God's
will should be sought.

Paul's vision is for a community wholly committed
to God's will. How far is this vision realised in our
Christian community?

COLOSSIANS 1:12–14
All change

Most people tend to resist changes. But some changes are necessary. Paul thinks of some which are indispensable for a life of true happiness.

Change of environment
An inheritance is prepared for believers. Paul calls it an inheritance of the saints in light. It vividly contrasts with our existing environment of darkness.

Change of status
Christians receive a qualification they did not possess before. This is not earned but given. The heirs are a people of privilege, but their privilege is wholly through grace.

Change of allegiance
Here the transfer is from the dominion of darkness to the kingdom of God's beloved Son. No greater contrast can be imagined. We recognise God's victory over the spiritual enemy.

Change of attitude
In the old dominion, guilt is rife. Man cannot escape from the consequences of sin. But now forgiveness is available. We can face God and face ourselves without fear. This is Paul's doctrine of redemption.

Paul is writing of an experience after which nothing is the same. Everything has to change. How foolish it is to resist such a beneficial change!

COLOSSIANS 1:15–23
Christ: who he is and what he does

This is one of Paul's most profound passages. We cannot reflect on it without being deeply impressed with his view of Christ. We may get lost in the depth of his statements, but we will be led to an attitude of wonder and worship.

His glorious person
Paul piles up here many significant phrases.

(a) *Image of the invisible.* Christ reveals God in a way otherwise unknowable.

(b) *First-born of all creation.* This shows his superiority to all creatures.

(c) *Creator of all things.* In him everything was created – this places him on an equality with God.

(d) *Upholder of all things.* In him everything holds together. This is a dynamic view of creation. It means that Christ is still active in it.

(e) *Head of the church.* Here is a sudden switch from the material creation to the new creation. Christ is dominant in the new community.

(f) *Beginning.* Perhaps an allusion to Christ as Alpha (as well as Omega). He is the initiator of salvation.

(g) *First-born from the dead.* This points at once to Christ's resurrection – the key to Christian truth.

(h) *Pre-eminent.* The uniqueness of Christ is an essential feature in Paul's thought. He can tolerate no comparison with others.

(i) *Fullness of God.* This expression can be understood only as an affirmation of deity.

His glorious achievements
Our understanding of Christ's person is only enhanced by what he has done.

(a) *He has reconciled everything.* It is surprising that

Paul speaks of 'things' here. It suggests that reconciliation of people affects all creation.

(b) *He has removed the obstacle between man and God.*
How? 'Through the blood of his cross', and 'in his
body of flesh through his death'. The cross has had a
profound result.

(c) *He will present his people holy and blameless to God.*
This is not merely a pious wish, but an assured result
of his death.

(d) *He has provided hope in the gospel.* Paul has been
called to proclaim Christ's doings. He conceives of
every creature hearing it. He wants the Colossians to
remain true to this gospel, since none can better it.

The true gospel centres in Christ and his work.
What does not exalt him is not the gospel. A study
of this passage should lead us into a clearer
understanding of the gospel.

COLOSSIANS 1:15–17
The glory of Christ

It is likely that at Colossae some had an inadequate
view of Christ. Certainly many still have a wrong
view. Paul proposes a view of Christ in relation to
God and in relation to the creation. These two
aspects form a good basis for understanding
Christian truth.

In relation to God
Paul's description can be viewed in two ways.

(a) *Representation.* How do we know God? Jesus said
that whoever had seen him had seen the Father
(John 12:45). Paul's idea of image here is similar. No
one can see God and live except the one who sees
Christ, who is his image.

(b) *Revelation*. The invisible makes himself known. Christ is seen as essentially the same as God himself.

In relation to creation

Paul sees the importance of Christ's position in the natural world.

(a) *The first-born*. This does not mean that Christ is no more than a creature. He is supreme in creation.

(b) *The agent*. Christ is the one through whom creation took place. He is the beginning or first principle of creation.

(c) *The object*. All things were created through him and *for* him. All we see was planned to glorify Christ.

(d) *The support*. Creation has not been left to chance. In him all things hold together. Paul sees Christ as providing stability.

Christ is at once our introduction to a knowledge of God and also to a knowledge of the real purpose behind creation.

COLOSSIANS 1:18–20
The supremacy of Christ in the church

The supremacy of Christ is a frequently recurring theme in Paul's letters. His view of the church is dictated by it.

He is its head
Clearly as head he controls the church.

He is its first principle
The word 'beginning' seems to point to the source from which all else springs.

He is its pattern of resurrection
The first is a sample and guarantee of others to follow.

He is the universal reconciler
Tension and enmity are alien to God. Christ's mission and death are designed to reverse the process.

We cannot too often reflect on the supremacy of Christ. It is a constant challenge both to individual Christians and to communities.

COLOSSIANS 1:18
The headship of Christ

In the body the head is in control. The members must obey the dictates of the head. Paul is using this illustration to show the importance of Christ.

What is involved in the headship of Christ?
Paul uses the body image elsewhere to illustrate the interdependence of members of the church on one another (Rom. 12; 1 Cor. 12).

Consider the relationship of Christ to his church.

He originates it.
He redeems it.
He sustains it.

What responsibilities are involved for the church?
In the physical body the members recognise the authority of the head. No member is allowed to usurp that authority. Every member must honour the head and joyfully accept direction.

In the church the members must unite in love to bring the greatest glory to the head.

What should be the result of Christ's headship?
Paul claims that Christ must have the pre-eminence. This is expressed comprehensively – in all things.

It applies especially within the church. But in view of Christ's part in creation it must also apply to the world.

The church has been weakened by a lack of appreciation of the truth of Christ's headship. Where that is firmly established the church cannot be dominated by human opinions.

COLOSSIANS 1:19
The fullness of God

This is an unexpected idea. Nothing else than fullness could be appropriate to God. But fullness points to its opposite – emptiness.

The nature of the fullness of God
It is difficult to grasp what Paul means. But something like the totality of godhead is in view. He does not think of Jesus Christ simply as divine. He implies a great deal more than that.

The fullness indwelling a man
In no more effective way could Paul indicate that Jesus was God incarnate. We note that there is no time element – the indwelling is permanent.

The indwelling fullness and the pleasure of God
What astonishes us here is that the whole Godhead is delighted with the incarnation. It was through this that God in Christ made peace through the cross.

Here is an inexhaustible theme. We cannot praise God enough that in a mysterious way his fullness dwelt in a man.

COLOSSIANS 1:21–23
Comprehensive reconciliation

*Paul has been writing about the reconciliation of
all things. But here he becomes more personal.
God's plans are never so sweeping that the
individual is overlooked. Paul thinks here of the
past, the present and the future.*

The past – what we were
There is value in looking back sometimes to recall the state
of affairs from which we have been delivered.

(a) *Alienated.* An alien is one who does not belong. He
does not share the benefits of citizenship. The natural man does not want to have fellowship with God.
He is not at home with God. This state of affairs has
been brought about through sin.

(b) *Hostile in mind.* This is the natural sequel to alienation. Paul speaks of the carnal mind as hostile
(Rom. 8:7). Man does not take kindly to God's
demands until faith enlightens him. Reconciliation
involves the removal of past hostility.

The present – what we are
When hostility is removed, we cease to resist God. There is
no longer any barrier, but the possibility of mutual love.

The basis of reconciliation is the cross. Paul speaks of 'his
body of flesh by his death'. It is clear that God has taken the
initiative. This is an objective basis for constant reconciliation.

The future – what we shall be
We are to be presented holy, blameless and irreproachable.
However weak and inadequate we may feel now, Paul
wants us to look to the future.

The whole plan of God is aimed to produce a community
of holy people. A future perspective is indispensable for the
Christian.

Yet note the conditions:

(a) *Continuance in the faith.* This does not mean human effort, but a continuing reliance on God.

(b) *Stability.* Christians dwell in the midst of moving currents. How is stability possible? It is centred in the gospel, not in oneself. The gospel is not open to change. It is still the same gospel that Paul preached.

Christians can and should be liberated people.
They have been reconciled to God.

COLOSSIANS 1:24–29
Rejoicing in suffering

The idea seems strange. How can affliction lead to joy? Paul is not masochistic or stoical towards pain. He is enunciating a spiritual principle, which he does with convincing reasons.

Because he was suffering for others

What he passed through was 'for your sake'. This puts a different complexion on hardship.

Paul's missionary work was fraught with dangers. Yet he constantly rejoiced over those who were reached with the gospel.

Because his sufferings were connected with Christ's

He actually says he is making up the deficiencies. He cannot mean that Christ's sufferings needed his to become effective.

Paul is thinking of the close identity between Christ and his people in the afflictions they endure. He sees his own sufferings as an extension of Christ's.

Because his sufferings were the result of his office

The sufferings were in a church context. Paul was a minister to make known God's word. He sees this as a divine office, whatever hardships were involved in it.

Moreover, the mystery is now made known. Paul refers to 'the riches of the glory of it'. To proclaim this, sufferings become of little importance.

Paul speaks of proclaiming, warning, teaching, toiling and striving – all to present people mature in Christ.

It is all a matter of perspective. Paul has so great a view of the nature of his task that present afflictions can actually become a matter of rejoicing.

COLOSSIANS 1:25–29
Paul's view of the ministry

This section focusses on several important aspects of the ministry. These aspects are still relevant for us today.

The ministry is a divine office
Here Paul reflects his consciousness of God's calling. This means his task is not of his own making. He was constantly under orders from above.

The ministry was to make known God's word
There was no question of Paul working up his message. He had received the gospel as much as he had received his office.

The ministry was centred in a mystery
This was not in the sense of a secret society, but in the sense of a message which God had to unlock. The gospel is made known, but is still a mystery to the unbelieving world.

Only the Christian can recognise the glory and know how great it is. Paul calls it 'Christ in you the hope of glory'.

The ministry involved much toil and energy
Paul did not sit back and expect God to work. Note the ceaseless activity suggested by versus 28, 29. Yet even so Paul does not rely on his own energy. God provides abundant strength for the task.

The ministry was to produce mature people

There is no denying the aim is high. Paul is thinking of everyone, not just some people of special spiritual calibre. The ministry is not complete until all are mature in Christ.

With such a view of his calling, it is no wonder that Paul thought lightly of the hardships involved. We need to compare our evaluation of the task of spreading the gospel.

COLOSSIANS 1:28, 29
Christian preaching

If we want to know what Christian preaching ought to be, we cannot have a better guide than Paul. He speaks out of a rich experience. We shall do well to note what he says.

Its subject is Christ

Paul has spoken of the mystery as 'Christ in you'. He is the one to be proclaimed.

Its sphere is everyone

Paul mentions every man three times. He has no place for selective preaching.

Its methods are varied

Proclamation, warning and teaching reflect this variety. We are reminded of Paul's great adaptability.

Its goal is transformation

No one is mature or complete. Yet this is the aim. Paul does not doubt that such transformation is possible.

The principles which Paul enunciates are timeless because the gospel is the same and the needs of people are the same.

COLOSSIANS 2:1–7
How to avoid delusion

In Paul's time there were specious talkers. This is an ever-present danger. The way to avoid being deluded by the false is to be thoroughly acquainted with the genuine. Paul gives some pointers in this direction.

Christian associations

Paul brings out the strong links between himself and Christians he has never met. He strives for them – the Colossians and the Laodiceans and others.

In Christ there is a strong bond of fellowship. This realisation should act as a barrier against delusion. Paul sees himself as with them in spirit (verse 5). There is mutual rejoicing over firmness of faith.

Christian encouragements

The knitting together of Christians in love is another safeguard. But love is here linked with understanding. Moreover, the understanding must be assured.

Christians who seek the truth may reach such understanding. Mutual understanding is a necessary part of Christian stability.

Christian treasure

God's mystery is a treasure. In Christ are the treasures of wisdom and knowledge. Christians are in possession of the key, i.e. Christ himself.

Reflection on the unspeakable value of our treasure will fortify us against any lesser alternatives.

Christian security

Paul reflects on the Christian's roots. The basis of his life is in Christ. This goes with being strengthened in him.

It should be noted that Paul links receiving and continuing here. There is a necessary progression.

With such a firm basis, the Christian should be well fortified to resist fine sounding, but deceiving arguments.

COLOSSIANS 2:1–3
Paul's unseen friends

This letter is an excellent example of Paul's attitude to those he had never met. He is as diligent in his concern for them as he is for those among whom he has worked.

A personal concern

Paul writes about his struggles on behalf of the churches in the Lycus valley. He uses a strong word, as if to liken it to the stress of an athlete in a contest.

Such intense concern deepens the fellowship between those who are absent from each other. This statement shows that lack of personal acquaintance does not exclude real fellowship between Christians.

A strong encouragement

Paul's prayer for these unknown Christians is expansive. He wants for them encouragement and unity. He uses the idea of being knit together in love. He clearly thinks of a very strong bond.

He also wants for them increasing understanding. Here is a striking combination of emotion and mind. Again Paul shows whole-heartedness in his words – he talks of full understanding.

A mystery revealed

The gospel is not secret. It appears to be hidden, but God has now made it known. Paul's desire is that all his friends should know the treasures which are found in Christ. There are no restrictions. The gospel treasure is for all who want it.

There is a rich content in Paul's prayer. It should challenge us to examine the quality of our own prayers for others.

COLOSSIANS 2:3
The treasures of wisdom

This statement challenges us to evaluate what is most important in life.

A right understanding of treasure
We live in a materialistic age in which what is most treasured is so often material wealth. Few would value wisdom more highly than wealth. But Christian values are on a different level.

The essence of spiritual treasure
This consists of wisdom and knowledge. Treasures of the mind are more valuable than those of the pocket. Wisdom leads to more understanding. When shared it increases rather than diminishes.

The source of all spiritual treasure
Paul talks of everything being hidden in Christ. He is the key to unlock true wisdom. In 1 Cor. 1:30 Paul speaks of Christ our wisdom. Such wisdom is too great to evaluate.

Every Christian is incomparably rich in Christ. Do we live as though we are spiritually wealthy?

COLOSSIANS 2:5–7
Possibilities in Christ

It is essential for Christians to know something of the potential there is in the Christian life. Paul helps here with some suggestions.

Stability
Paul rejoices over his readers on two grounds.
  (a) Because of their *orderliness*. This suggests good Christian discipline.

189

(b) Because of their *firmness*. They had not moved away from their faith.

Such qualities are possible for all Christians.

Growth

Having believed in Christ, there is need for development. Roots are important, for growth depends on them.

Here Christ is seen as the soil (in Eph. 3:17 it is love). The metaphor then changes to that of a building.

But the idea is the same. Faith must never be static. Growth and stability are co-existent.

Thanksgiving

Paul places great store on thanksgiving in his letters. Here he shows the possibility of abounding in it. He never thinks in stinting terms of God's love.

Christians should never run out of themes for praising God.

These three qualities are but a selection of the possibilities open to us. If we realise these, they will open the way for further discoveries.

COLOSSIANS 2:6, 7
The walk of the believer

Paul often uses the word 'walk' to describe the way of life. It is suggestive because it implies deliberate choices involving manner and direction.

The walk must be related to Christ

For the Christian the whole of life should be Christ-centred. The idea of living 'in him' may seem mystical, but Christ is the source of the Christian's strength.

Clearly only those who have received him can walk with him. It should be noted that Paul stresses here an acceptance of the Lordship of Christ.

The walk must be consistent

Rooted, built up, and established – all point to reliability. Christian living is not like a see-saw. Stability is an essential quality. The faith is not movable. The gospel is not affected by change.

The walk must be joyful

It should be evident to others. Thankfulness is contagious. There cannot be too much of it. It banishes grumbling and discontent.

Walking in Christ is both possible and desirable. How does our manner of life match up to it?

COLOSSIANS 2:8–15
Christ and man's philosophy

There has always been tension between man's intellectual ideas and God's revelation. Such tension existed at Colossae. Here Paul sets out both the negative and the positive aspects.

Any philosophy is suspect which leads away from Christ

The yardstick is whether the teaching is according to Christ. Paul's descriptions are informative.

(a) *Philosophy* was a general word for human systems of thought. Paul is not here decrying human thought, but is denying its right to judge Christ.

(b) *Empty deceit* contrasts with the fullness found in Christ. Again Christ is the measure against which other ideas must be assessed.

(c) *Human tradition* probably referred to the over-emphasis on tradition among the Jews. But it contains a universal caution against relying on tradition.

(d) *The elemental spirits* seems to be a reference to the

spirit-world which was believed to influence the natural world.

Paul is warning against everything which is not Christ-centred.

Christ by contrast is seen as the fullness of God
It cannot be denied that this is a high view of Christ.

It presents a mystery – full godhead dwelling in a human form. It is no wonder man's ingenuity had never thought of this. Paul must have reached this conclusion through revelation.

Christ has become the head of his people
The head controls the members. Moreover the head pours fullness of life into the members.

This strongly contrasts with the emptiness of human philosophy. Paul's use of the fullness–emptiness comparison is clearly intentional.

Christ is the true sign of his people's standing
For the Jew circumcision was the hallmark.

But Christians have a sign which is not an external rite (made with hands). For Paul this was a real spiritual alternative.

Christ has overcome all man's problems
  (a) He has raised the believer to newness of life.
  (b) He has forgiven our sins. Paul actually speaks of trespass – stepping aside from God's true path.
  (c) He has cancelled all legal obligations. Paul sees this as being effected through the cross.
  (d) He has triumphed over all spiritual enemies.

In this way Paul brings out the superiority of Christ over all man's ideas. Current issues may now be different, but nothing has changed the superior status of Christ.

COLOSSIANS 2:8
A warning against speculative thinkers

Paul was concerned to deal with a particular wrong thinking which was affecting the Colossians. But his advice has a more general application.

The kind of speculation condemned
Paul calls it empty deceit. The idea is of teaching which is hollow. It was based on man's ideas rather than God's.

Man-centred presentations of Christianity have always failed to avoid emptiness because they are based on speculation rather than on revelation.

The origin of the speculation
It was according to human tradition. It was not based on divinely authenticated sources.

It did not go back to God. Some tradition can preserve truth. But it cannot inaugurate truth. Only God can do that.

The pseudo-spiritual nature of the speculation
Appeal to the elementary spirits shows some attempt to explain the universe in non-material terms. But these were in competition with God.

The challenge in the face of such speculation
A danger signal 'beware' is sounded. The warning is against those who would carry off the readers as if they were booty. Speculation is always on the lookout for gullible 'prey'.

Paul had no doubt had experience of many being deluded. History can provide multitudes of examples. This makes it imperative for every Christian to take heed.

COLOSSIANS 2:9, 10
Christ the fullness of the Godhead

This is a profound theological statement, but it will richly repay thought even if at the end we are still perplexed by the depth of it.

What fullness meant to Christ

It did not mean a spiritual presence, since Paul uses the word 'bodily'. Christ was both true man and true God. God was with him and in him.

We are faced here with the mystery of the incarnation.

What fullness means to us

There is a direct connection between Christ's being filled with God's fullness and the Christian's fullness of life.

Because he is filled, those in him can have a fuller life in him.

How Christ's fullness and our fullness can be explained

It is because he is head of his people and sovereign over all other rule and authority.

His word is absolute. Those in him share the same life.

How God can fully dwell in man will always remain a mystery. The more we ponder it the more it baffles us. Yet we can and should experience the fullness.

194

COLOSSIANS 2:11–15
Acceptance, forgiveness and triumph

How a person is to approach God and relate to him is an age-old question. The Jews relied on ritual procedures like circumcision, which were in fact based on the Old Testament. But the Christian revelation presents a different view.

Acceptance

Paul talks of a circumcision not made with hands. He then identifies it as the circumcision of Christ. He is clearly not meaning an external act. Indeed, the body of flesh is to be put off.

This is Paul's way of saying that the external rite is not necessary for salvation. Acceptance is through identification with Christ – hence the reference to baptism and being raised with him.

Forgiveness

When God makes alive he gives pardon for past sins. Death and sin go together, as do life and forgiveness. The record of our trespasses is obliterated.

The bond of which Paul writes is an acknowledgement of debt in the debtor's handwriting. It was legally binding. The idea of nailing it to the cross vividly brings out the nature of forgiveness. It is as if the cross declares 'no more debts'.

Triumph

If the principalities and powers are evil powers, Paul affirms they are defeated foes. If, as some think, they are good agencies (angels), the public spectacle would make their position clear.

But the first interpretation is the more likely. Paul seems to be thinking of a conqueror bringing his defeated enemies

with him. God's mission in Christ is a marvellously successful rescue operation.

*Christians need to be reminded that God has the
final victory, whatever men may say.*

COLOSSIANS 2:16–23
Errors and their antidote

*Wrong ideas arose at an early stage in Christian
history. Deviations of one sort or another are
always present. This makes Paul's advice to the
Colossians still relevant to us.*

Legalism

The type of religion which requires no more than adher-
ence to certain regulations is totally misleading. Yet many
feel happier with a code of rules.

This approach nevertheless detracts from Christ. Feast
days and festivals are mere shadows compared with Christ.

Angel-worship

Many ancients revered angels, but in the church this was
unacceptable, since God alone should be worshipped. The
worshippers were showing humility, but they were worshipping the wrong objects. Their humility was therefore
spurious.

They were claiming visions and were proud of themselves – another evidence that the humility was not true.
Paul calls them sensuous.

Wherever these conditions are evident, there is something false, however sincere the worshippers appear to be.
Paul sees it as a poor alternative to worshipping and being
united to Christ the head.

Asceticism

Another kind of error which creeps into religious observ-
ance is rigorous asceticism. This is the kind of self-help in

which self-denial forms the main means of achieving one's aims.

Here there were regulations about things. It all seemed very religious and very rigorous. The aim was to subdue the body.

But Paul attaches little importance to such regulations. Those for whom Christ died know a better way.

We need constant reminders of the dangers in living according to our own efforts which can lead only to error. Paul's antidote is to centre everything in Christ.

COLOSSIANS 2:16–19
Beware of these people

Paul's epistles are full of warnings. Many are about people who would have an adverse influence on the church. In this passage two types are in mind.

Beware the self-appointed judges

There is one class of people who set themselves up as critics. They think they know and therefore have a right to judge. The case Paul mentions was concerned with feast days and festivals. This was an easy subject for legalism.

Paul advises
(a) Let no one judge you in such matters.
(b) Recognise these things as mere shadows.

Beware the unspiritually minded

Some discernment is here needed. On the surface some spiritual qualities (like humility) are apparent. But they are misleading (as in the worship of angels).

The real test is whether a person gets puffed up. Those convinced of their own importance are dangerous. They may be purveyors of idle notions. They cause others to be disqualified.

Such pseudo-spiritual mindedness can have many facets. Christians need to be able to distinguish the true from the false.

The main test is contact with the head. If the teachers are not glorifying Christ, they are not part of the body.

Paul's body metaphor is seen to have a very practical purpose. God causes the true body to grow. Beware of any who would impede that growth.

COLOSSIANS 2:16, 17
Don't chase after shadows

In the physical world it is not difficult to differentiate between shadow and substance. The former always presupposes the latter. The object is more important than its shadow.

Shadows mistaken for substance
Paul writes about those who overemphasise the importance of meats and of feasts and festivals – i.e. ritual observances.

In spiritual experience ritualism has often been mistaken for the real thing.

Shadows eclipsed by substance
No sensible person is content with shadows. But what is the substance?

Paul points to Christ. There is nothing shadowy about him.

Those with a true view of Christ will attach little value to ritual observances. There is something so much better.

COLOSSIANS 2:18, 19
Against angel worship

Although this aspect of worship was considered valid among some of the Colossians, it has no direct modern counterpart. Nevertheless Paul's warnings on the matter are relevant to all kinds of alternative worship which detract from the worship of Christ.

Angel worship is condemned

Since angels are creatures, worship of them is a challenge to the worship of God. God is jealous over his right to be worshipped.

He will not allow any alternative. In Hebrews Christ's superiority to angels is a major theme (cf. Heb. 1 and 2).

Angel worship falsely purports to encourage humility

The argument probably was that man needed an intermediary because of his own weakness.

But when the intermediary attracts the worship, the humility becomes suspect. Believers have direct, not indirect, access to God.

Angel worship is linked with visions

The Colossian teachers were evidently ecstatics. Those who claim visions can rarely avoid being puffed up. The whole exercise easily becomes a slave to the senses.

What Paul says here about angel worship may be illustrated from modern types of Christianity which rely on emotion rather than reason.

Angel worship robs people

Because their worship is deflected from Christ, they become disqualified. They cannot gain the true reward which comes to those who serve Christ.

Worshipping any alternative to God not only robs God of what is his due, but robs the believer.

By way of contrast Paul points to Christ as head of the body which is the church. No one is ever said to

*grow in relation to an angelic being. Christ is so
clearly superior.*

COLOSSIANS 2:20–23
Religious regulations and their dangers

*The preference for regulations rather than for
spiritual challenges is common in all ages. The
reason for this preference is that it is easier. But
Paul clearly sees the dangers.*

Christ has changed our approach to regulations

In his death he has overcome the elemental spirits. He lifts
us out of our environment by setting us free from its claims
upon us.

Paul talks of 'regulations' in connection with the 'world'.
Christians are expected to have an entirely different
approach. They must not be in bondage to them.

Human regulations are summed up as taboos

The examples which Paul cites relate to touch and to taste.
These are purely sensory experiences. Their negative
aspect contrasts strongly with the positive Christian relationship to Christ.

Paul thinks of the ascetics as acting according to human
precepts and doctrines.

Regulations cannot check sensuous indulgence

On the surface they appear to be good. Rigorous self-
discipline draws out certain admiration. Ascetics in all ages
have sought to gain favour with God through this means.

*Christian discipline should be prompted by love of
Christ rather than by a slavish obedience to
regulations.*

COLOSSIANS 3:1–4
Risen with Christ

The resurrection of Christ is central to the Christian faith. It provides the power for Christian living. Whatever applies to Christ applies also to the Christian. Our sights are at once on a higher level.

The higher nature
A believer lives life on a higher plane. His aims must be on higher things. His mind is controlled by higher standards. This, at least, is the ideal.

Paul urges a definite resolve towards this end. 'Things above' means things controlled by God. 'Things that are on earth' means things pursued without reference to God.

The hidden resources
Such high ideals seem impossible. After all believers must still live on the earth. But help is given to maintain a right balance.

Our life is hidden in God. We have resources unknown to those who merely live for earthly things. In some senses Christians are constantly discovering new spiritual strength they did not suspect.

The hope for glory
Life here is not the end. Greater things are in store. The appearing of Christ in glory is a major focus for the future.

Since the coming will be glorious, so will those who are with Christ be glorious. This is the transformation theme which is frequent in Paul (cf. Phil. 3:20, 21).

The Christian has an obligation to develop higher standards than those adopted by the world. He is given strong incentives to do so.

COLOSSIANS 3:1, 2
Minds on higher things

The bent of a person's mind determines his actions. Here Paul is speaking of the Christian mind.

It is based on our resurrection with Christ.
Since Christ is exalted to God's right hand, the believer has an obligation to live and think worthily. If we are raised with him we must think his thoughts. Our union with Christ has an ennobling effect.

It means a deliberate raising of standards
There is a positive injunction to seek higher things. This does not come naturally. There is an antipathy between earthly and heavenly patterns of thinking.

When thought is Christ-centred, action will be Christ-honouring. We have a strong motive for examining our thought patterns.

COLOSSIANS 3:3, 4
The hidden life

When Jesus lived on earth people could see him. After the resurrection, only believers encountered him. As far as the world as a whole was concerned he had vanished. There is still a 'hidden' aspect of Christ.

Christian life is a hidden life
The non-Christian world cannot appreciate the source of the Christian's strength.

The union with Christ, the empowering to grow more

like him, the different standards, are all an enigma to the world. But they are the Christian's lifeline.

It is hidden with Christ in God
The life of Jesus is an excellent example of life in God. He lived in the consciousness of doing God's will and speaking God's mind.

Our hidden life links us with the same source.

It is hidden now, but will be revealed later
It is not an eternal secret. It is due for public attestation.

Christ our life will one day appear. What seems hidden now will then be gloriously seen.

We cannot expect the non-Christian world to recognise our immense resources, but some of the effects should be visible. We are heading for glory.

COLOSSIANS 3:4
Appearing with Christ

Paul is frequently pointing to the coming of Christ. He sees this as the great hope of the future.

The certainty of Christ's appearing
Paul does not debate the possibility. He affirms the fact. Jesus predicted his own coming.

What Paul says only underlines this coming event. It is the concluding event of the age.

The significance of Christ's appearing
The appearing is not simply a Christ event. Since he is our life, we are all implicated.

We will naturally be affected when our life-source appears again to wind up this age.

The glory of Christ's appearing
The glory is shared. Christ's glory is especially seen in Rev.

1 and 19. But here Paul thinks of a change for believers to a glorious state.

In 1 Cor. 15:52, 53 he writes of the change from perishable to imperishable.

Belief in the second coming of Christ has practical implications. Those destined for glory must examine their present walk.

COLOSSIANS 3:5–14
A change of clothing

The idea of garments to express spiritual truths is not new. Cf. the reference to the high priest's filthy garments in Zech. 3. The returning prodigal received a change of clothing.
Paul uses the metaphor here of a new wardrobe which involves casting away the old clothes.

The old garments

Paul describes them in a general way as 'earthly'. They relate to the way people live without God.

(a) *Sensuality*. Paul provides four descriptions of this.
 1. *Immorality* is a general term for sexual sin.
 2. *Impurity* describes the mental and spiritual aspect.
 3. *Passion* is a stronger word to express the driving force behind it.
 4. *Evil desire* shows a complete absence of standards of goodness or respect in sexual matters.

(b) *Covetousness*. Paul qualifies this as idolatry. This centres on a materialistic approach to life. It suggests a greedy, self-opinionated attitude.

Covetousness is attractive to the natural man, but becomes tawdry to the spiritually enlightened.

(c) *Sins of heart and lip*. Paul thinks here of wrong attitudes which lead to wrong speech.

'Anger and wrath' are outbursts of self-centred passion. Since these must have some outlet in speech, Paul mentions 'slander', 'malice' and 'foul talk', all of which show lack of self-control. He then adds another – 'falsehood', which springs from a lack of respect towards God and men.

These old garments are seen to be unacceptable to Christians. They must be discarded.

The new garments

Paul is never negative. With 'put off' he must add 'put on'. He refers to the new nature, which is linked to the image of the creator. He mentions some of the Christian's new clothes.

(a) *Compassion and kindness.* Jesus was the supreme example of both these qualities. Paul is here thinking of active qualities which spring into action. Both qualities have a powerful effect on others.

(b) *Humility and meekness.* Neither of these comes naturally to most people. Yet they are garments which need putting on. Jesus claimed to be meek and lowly (Matt. 11:29).

(c) *Forbearance and love.* There is no place for arrogance or self-esteem. A forgiving spirit paves the way for love. Paul sees love as a kind of cloak which binds the rest together.

Anyone arrayed in these new garments cannot fail to be noticed. How complete has our change of clothing been?

COLOSSIANS 3:5–11
Mortification

Paul points us to the need for mortification – a putting to death of whatever is earthly. This is the negative part of the process of sanctification.

An effort is needed to deal with the earthly
Until conversion most people regard the earthly as normal. We are constantly relating to our present environment. But after conversion, different standards apply.

This requires a clean break with the past standards. Putting them to death seems drastic. But Paul knew the need for a crisis. In Christ we have already died.

Some sample areas for mortification are suggested
The sins mentioned were rife in Gentile society. Sexual sins, selfish sins, angry communications were all characteristic.

They are obviously all inappropriate for the Christian. Moreover they incur God's wrath (verse 6).

Mortification must be linked with sanctification
Putting off is only one side of it. The new nature replaces the old nature. It has already happened.

Once the old is discarded, the process of renewal begins. The pattern is nothing less than the image of God.

Distinctions disappear when mortification takes place
Paul mentions several widely held distinctions which no longer exist in Christ.
  (a) *National*. The deep Jewish–Gentile rift is healed.
  (b) *Religious*. Circumcision is no longer a yard-stick of orthodoxy.
  (c) *Social*. Divisions of men into classes, like barbarians, Scythians, slaves, freeman, are no longer valid.

Why? Because Christ is all and in all. When this is grasped the sins mentioned are seen to be unacceptable.

A deliberate act of putting to death is not easy. But the Christian has no alternative. If he has died with Christ, his sins must die with him.

COLOSSIANS 3:8, 9
Inward and outward social sins

Paul is not content to be vague about sin. He sees the value of being specific. He produces several lists of sins, which may be regarded as samples. It is easier to ignore general statements than definite ones, and Paul has no intention that his readers should not take stock of what he says.

Sins of feeling

Anger need not be a sin (cf. Eph. 4:26), but it generally is a sin. It is based on the assumption that a person has a right to be resentful against others (or even against God), if something happens that does not please him.

That Paul has in mind the wrong kind of anger is clear from the link with *wrath*. To these are added *malice* which delights to hurt others. Malice is even more vicious than anger. It cannot coexist with Christian love.

Sins of speech

Wrong feelings soon lead to wrong words.

(a) *Slander* is an attack on another's reputation without justification. This is especially despicable when the other person has no opportunity to defend himself.

(b) *Coarse language* probably refers to language that is foul or filthy. This would include obscene language, but it refers more generally to all kinds of unwholesome speech.

(c) *Falsehood* is mentioned because lying is no part of

the new nature. If one's words cannot be relied on, true social communication breaks down.

All these sins invoke the divine displeasure. There is only one course of action for the Christian – to put them away

COLOSSIANS 3:11
The Christian and social distinctions

It is not easy for Christians to learn that Christ dispenses with social distinctions. Most of us bring into Christian life the barriers of our environment.

In Christ distinctions vanish
Paul propounds the principle that Christ is all and in all. The absolute supremacy of Christ has a devastating effect on social conventions.

If Christ is in everything, man-made distinctions have no relevance.

These distinctions are of various types
  (a) *National*. The Jew and the Gentile controversy is relevant to modern nationalistic movements.
  (b) *Religious*. Those who relied on ritual were no longer able to claim superiority. In fact, ritual is abolished in Christ as a means of winning favour with God.
  (c) *Cultural*. Civilisation has tended to split the world into a kind of cultural hierarchy. In Roman times, barbarians and Scythians were despised.
  (d) *Class*. The freeman–slave distinction ran deep in those days. Any form of class distinction is unacceptable in Christ.

The church needs to relearn this basic fact that in Christ all are one because Christ is all in all.

COLOSSIANS 3:12–17
Guidelines for Christian living

*Paul packs much positive advice into small space
in this passage. It repays the careful consideration
of all Christians. There are several important
qualities emphasised.*

Being compassionate

When Paul thinks of the Christian's new garments, the idea
of compassion and its kindred qualities spring to mind.

Such qualities as kindness, meekness and patience are
the exact opposite of the anger of verse 8. This whole group
demands consideration for others – an essential aspect of
Christian living.

Being forgiven

Among Christians forbearance is more important than the
asserting of rights. Others may wrong us, but a forgiving
spirit takes the sting out of it.

Jesus set a perfect example in forbearance (cf. Luke
23:34). Paul in fact cites the Lord's forgiveness as a pattern.

Being loving

Elsewhere Paul sets out the supremacy of love (cf. 1 Cor.
13). Here also he gives it priority. It has a binding effect.
Where love operates within a community Christians will
not fall out with each other. Instead there will be complete
harmony.

Being peaceful

Christians who are united will also show a calm and serene
approach. But it comes from Christ, not from themselves.

Indeed some conscious determination to allow God's
peace to rule is necessary.

Being thankful

If Christ's word dwells in us, spontaneous praise will result.
Paul links teaching with singing, a combination which has
marked Christian worship through the centuries.

But Paul shows the need for the right attitude (thankfulness in your hearts) behind the singing. Everything is to be done in the name of Jesus – a sure recipe for continuous praise.

Such a pattern for Christian living is a constant challenge. Are these the impressions we create on the minds of others?

COLOSSIANS 3:12–17
Christian patterns

The New Testament continually introduces contrasts between the Christian approach to life and the non-Christian approach. Here Paul explains the new way of life against the background of the old.

New patterns of love
The Christian is not dominated by erotic forms of love nor by mere emotionalism. Christian love is on a much higher level and makes stringent demands.

(a) *Compassion* shows love reaching out to the unfortunate. In a violent age compassion is not highly prized.

(b) *Kindness* is an attitude of mind which values others.

(c) *Humility and meekness* are the opposite of self-assertion and self-importance.

(d) *Forbearance and forgiveness* combine tolerance of others with a willingness to forget faults. Here Paul cites the supreme pattern – as the Lord forgave.

(e) *Love* is seen as the binding principle.

New patterns of harmony
Most long for peace, but history demonstrates how difficult it is to achieve. The world is full of discord rather than concord.

But Christian peace is something different. It springs

from a new inner principle – the peace of Christ acting as an umpire. The idea is that anything that challenges the peace of Christ should be ruled out. This principle provides a valuable rule in moral decisions.

New patterns of worship

Paul enumerates certain features which are essential to Christian worship.

(a) *Receiving the word.* This is specifically the word of Christ. The Christian must listen to his voice. It is to be received richly – i.e. in all its fullness and variety.

(b) *Teaching and admonishing.* This is a valuable exercise in the sharing of wisdom. Paul's words do not presuppose a one-man ministry.

(c) *Singing psalms and hymns.* All spiritual awakenings burst into song. Paul recognised the value of it at an early stage. What the hymns and songs were we do not know – but they were presumably praise to God.

New patterns of action

It is revolutionary to do everything and say everything 'in the name of the Lord Jesus'. This wipes out all self-interest. Everything becomes Christ-centred.

> *The new man in Christ is called on to examine his patterns of behaviour. Radical changes are certainly needed.*

COLOSSIANS 3:12–14
A change of wardrobe

*The metaphor of dress is suggestive. People obtain
new garments for a variety of reasons – to be
fashion conscious, to out-do others or simply
because the old has worn out.*
*Paul has vividly demonstrated the unattractiveness
of the old ways (verses 5–9) and has declared
God's displeasure over them. But something must
take their place.*

A change is necessary because of a new status
Christians are described in a threefold way.
  (a) *God's chosen ones.* This is a frequent theme in Paul.
      What God has chosen is precious in his sight.
  (b) *Holy.* All believers are called 'saints' (holy ones).
      This shows what they are called to be.
  (c) *Beloved.* Jesus was called God's beloved, and the
      same word is applied to believers. It speaks of special
      love.
Such privileged people need a suitable spiritual wardrobe.

The new wardrobe is full of excellent virtues
All the virtues named are an intensification of what may at
times be considered natural graces.
  (a) *Compassion and kindness* are manifested in some
      non-Christian circles, but they are not the norm.
  (b) *Humility and meekness and patience* are not highly
      prized in a competitive world. To many meekness is
      equivalent to weakness. But for the Christian it is
      expected.
  (c) *Forbearance and forgiveness* means a readiness to
      overlook injury or insult. Jesus advised a 490-times
      level of forgiveness (Matt. 18:22).

*There is no denying that Christians who are
arrayed with these virtues will be noticed.*

COLOSSIANS 3:18–4:1
Christian relationships

The Christian faith has a powerful effect on human relationships. Paul cites three examples and gives advice on each.

Husbands and wives

Paul's advice to women to submit to their husbands has often been misunderstood. It must be recognised that he is writing in a Christian context. 'As is fitting in the Lord' is a reminder of this.

But this is valid only in the light of Paul's advice to husbands. Love must dominate its relationship, which renders invalid any talk of 'rights' within the marriage relationship.

Parents and children

Here again the determining factor is what pleases the Lord. Obedience to parents is important for the maintenance of discipline and the development of character.

But again there are conditions. Fathers must act in a responsible way – not provoking.

A truly Christian domestic scene requires love and understanding on the part of all concerned. Paul does not deal with the problem of irresponsible parents, of broken homes, or of indiscipline. His purpose is to provide a positive pattern.

Masters and servants

Paul is addressing himself to a situation in which slavery was an accepted social system. He advises slaves to obey, bearing in mind that their real service is to the Lord. His advice might seem hard where masters were cruel and irresponsible.

But Paul expresses a spiritual principle – you serve the Lord and not men. This must affect everyone's attitude to work. Any injustices should be left in God's hands.

Such an ethic may seem inadequate in modern industrial relations, but in Paul's time there was no real alternative.

Masters who are Christians have an obligation to act fairly. The heavenly analogy is a powerful restraint on Christian employers.

The Christian revolution from within transformed family life and helped to lessen social tensions. Those who would expect a more radical challenge should reflect on whether spiritual methods could not achieve more than political means.

COLOSSIANS 3:18–21
Christian family life

It may be that some in Colossae undervalued family life. Certainly this is true of the modern world. There has been a deplorable break-up of family relationships. Paul points the way for a Christian model.

Duties are reciprocal
Paul addresses each group in turn and each is seen to have duties appropriate to itself. It is clear that each depends on the other doing its part.

Principles are simple
Paul did not believe in complicated exhortations. Wives 'submit', husbands 'love', children 'obey', fathers 'do not provoke'.

Some may consider the advice to be over-simplified. But Paul believes in stating basic principles.

Motives are spiritual
Much family life breaks down through lack of a sufficient motive to sustain harmony. But the Christian reasons for good family relations are concerned with the Lord.

What is fitting in the Lord, or what pleases the Lord is the dominant consideration.

These principles place family life on a firm footing. The Christian pattern is for a family to be united in pleasing the Lord.

COLOSSIANS 3:22–4:1
A Christian approach to employment

Although the contemporary situation was dominated by slavery, which no longer applies in the same sense in the modern world, some of Paul's teaching on this subject still has relevance.

True service
Paul brings out three characteristics for Christians in a work situation.

(a) *Obedience.* This involves an attitude of responsibility.

(b) *Conscientiousness.* Paul advises against 'eye-service' – doing things merely to be noticed. He recommends rather singleness of mind.

(c) *Wholeheartedness.* Paul urges hearty workmanship, by which he means that Christians should enjoy what they do.

True management
So often bad relations are caused by wrong attitudes on the part of the bosses.

Management which is run on Christian lines needs a code of practice which ensures justice and fairness. Masters (and employers) have this responsibility.

The motive behind both
Whether slave or master, employee or employer, Christ-

ians are governed by their relation to Christ (cf. 3:24; 4:1). Whatever we do, we must do it as a service to Christ.

Also both groups are answerable to God who will give either reward or retribution. This is a powerful sanction.

> *Modern industry is not run on Christian principles. But Christians are not absolved from the responsibility of acting on them.*

COLOSSIANS 4:2–6
Advice to Christians

> *Here is a prisoner apostle writing to people he had never met. What he wrote has relevance to all Christians. It falls into two parts.*

Approach to God

Paul has much to say about prayer in his epistles. He gives samples in his own prayers for his various readers.

(a) *Prayer must be persistent.*

1. It requires effort. It is more than a habit. Paul suggests resolute application.

2. It involves watchfulness. Our spiritual enemies are always alert. Vigilance is essential.

3. It requires thankfulness. We should remind ourselves of what God has already done. Paul constantly urges thanksgiving.

(b) *Prayer must include others.*

'Pray for us' is a valuable antidote to introspective prayer.

1. An open door for the message. Consider the many closed doors today and pray specifically about them. But also rejoice over the doors which are open.

2. An opportunity to proclaim the mystery. It is because it is a mystery that prayer is needed.

Apologetics, organised campaigns, vigorous out-
reach, are all valuable. But a mystery requires an
act of God to unveil it.

3. A clear presentation. If the mystery is to be
   understood, a lucid exposition of the gospel is
   needed. Prayer reminds us of our dependence on
   God.

Approach to men

Paul gives some useful advice on approaching others.

(a) *Be wise*. This involves understanding others. It also
    presupposes tact. Much wisdom is required for
    everyday living.

(b) *Make the most of opportunities*. This means using the
    time to the full.

(c) *Watch conversation*. The way we speak is noticed by
    others. Hence the need for vigilance. Our conver-
    sation should be:

    1. Full of grace. This means reflecting the grace of
       God.
    2. Seasoned with salt. Ensuring wholesome words.
    3. Ready with adequate answers. This does not
       mean that Christians are expected to be know-
       alls. But there is a Christian answer to every
       situation.

*Pray for open doors and when they come pray for
the grace to make the most of the opportunities.*

COLOSSIANS 4:2
Prayer

Paul regards prayer as a duty, not as an option.

The duty of continual prayer

What does Paul mean? He cannot literally mean 'always'.
But the word must mean that a prayerful attitude should be
adopted, which will result in frequent prayer.

The duty of vigilance
We need to watch that prayer proceeds from the right attitudes and is applied to the right themes. Without vigilance prayer can become irrelevant.

The duty of thanksgiving
It may seem wrong to speak of duty. But in 2 Thess. 1:3, Paul implies this. We are obliged to remember to say 'Thank you' to God.

Paul makes high, but necessary, demands about prayer.

COLOSSIANS 4:3, 4
Praying for others

Most of Paul's prayers concentrate on others. This must be considered a firm principle for Christian prayer life.

Christians have a duty to pray for God's servants
'Pray for us' is a highly personal prayer. Paul does not suggest prayer in the abstract.

Such prayer should be specific
The request was for an open door – that people would have the opportunity to hear the gospel. It was a request for ability to explain the gospel.

Communication needs clarity, especially when the subject of proclamation is a mystery.

These prayer requests are samples. Paul the great apostle could not do without the prayer support of other Christians. The greatest can be supported by the prayers of the least.

COLOSSIANS 4:7–18
Paul and his associates

The ends of Paul's letters are often revealing of his relationships with others, and Colossians is specially interesting in this respect.

The two he sends with the letter
Paul names two people to be sent to Colossae.
  (a) *Tychicus*. He was possibly the scribe who wrote the letter. He was certainly the one who took it. Note Paul's description of him – beloved brother, faithful minister, fellow servant. He was a valued associate.
  (b) *Onesimus*. He too was faithful and beloved. And yet he was a runaway slave (cf. the epistle to Philemon). He was a Colossian.

Paul sees both these men as suitable representatives to report on his affairs.

The six who send greetings
The three Jewish Christians. These were the men of the circumcision (verse 11).
  (a) *Aristarchus* is described as a fellow-prisoner. He was with Paul on his journey to Rome (Acts 27:2). He appears to have been a Macedonian (Acts 20:4).
  (b) *Mark* deserted Paul on his first missionary journey, but he had now been fully restored.
  (c) *Jesus Justus* is not mentioned elsewhere in the New Testament.

Paul mentions what a comfort these three had been to him.
The three Gentile Christians.
  (d) *Epaphras* was a Colossian. He is described as a bond-slave of Jesus Christ. He prayed much for the maturity and assurance of his fellow Christians.
  (e) *Luke* is described simply as the beloved physician. He accompanied Paul on some of his journeys. He was with him when he wrote 2 Timothy (cf. 4:11).
  (f) *Demas* is not particularly commended here. He later forsook the apostle (2 Tim. 4:10).

Greetings for other churches

There are two groups included here:

(a) *Laodicea* became a prosperous, yet luke-warm, church according to Rev. 3.

(b) *Nympha's house church*. This may have been part of the Laodicean church or a church elsewhere.

Instructions for Colossae

Paul suggests an exchange of letters. This shows his appreciation of the value of the circulation of his letters.

There was also advice given regarding Archippus. The Colossians as a whole were to encourage him. He is mentioned in the letter to Philemon.

Concluding personal greeting

This was added in Paul's own handwriting. He gives a parting reminder about his chains.

There is something like a tapestry with several strands in this closing section. It throws light on the circle of people who surrounded Paul.

COLOSSIANS 4:10, 11
Three Jewish colleagues join in the greetings

We can learn much from the lesser characters in the New Testament.

Aristarchus

He was a Thessalonian (Acts 20:4). He was arrested at Ephesus while he was with Paul (Acts 19:29). He accompanied Paul to Rome (Acts 27:2). He is still with Paul as a fellow-prisoner.

Here is a man completely loyal to Paul. Hardship has strengthened rather than weakened his support. He was probably unknown to the Colossians. Out of suffering he sends greetings.

Mark
He had had a rather chequered association with Paul. He was a relative of Barnabas and a split had occurred because of him. He had left Paul during the first missionary journey. Paul's refusal to take him again seems reasonable.

But now confidence has been restored and he is with Paul again. Paul does not tell what instructions had been sent. We can only surmise that some may have hesitated to receive Mark. Paul shows his large-heartedness here.

Jesus Justus
Unlike the other two, this man is an unknown. Nevertheless Paul numbers him among his fellow-workers for the kingdom. He was as much a comfort to Paul as the others.

This lesser-known associate of the apostle has gone down in history simply as a Christian who sent greetings to a small unimportant community.

Never underrate the importance of lesser colleagues. Paul never did, and his example should be a spur to us.

COLOSSIANS 4:12, 13
Epaphras, a servant of Jesus Christ

This man was described as a servant of Jesus Christ. What we learn about him here can serve as a challenge to us.

He was one of them
As a Colossian he knew the situation from the inside.

He was a beloved fellow-servant with Paul
This speaks of Paul's warm affection for him.

He was a faithful minister of Christ
Paul uses the word 'faithful' in the sense of dependable.

He was a great intercessor
His prayers were constant. They were earnest. They were spiritual – for maturity and assurance.

He was a hard worker
His ministry touched three towns, Colossae, Laodicea and Hierapolis.

He was a good representative
He had reported on the Colossians' love in the Spirit.

Clearly Epaphras was a choice servant of God. He was a man after Paul's own heart.